BIGGER THAN BASKETBALL

THE DAYTON FLYERS' GREATEST SEASON

LARRY HANSGEN

Published in association with Per Capita Publishing, a division of Content Capital.

Cover photograph by Erik Schelkun.

ISBN 13: 978-1-954020-00-9

Photo Credits: Chapters 1, 2, 3, 4, 5, 6, 7, 9, 11, 15, 16, 19: Larry Hansgen. Chapter 8: Bill Meyers. Chapter 9: Cindy Carusone. Chapter 12: George Hellmund. Chapter 13: Mike Galbraith. Chapter 14: Henry Stark. Chapter 17: Melodie Bennett. Chapter 18: Erik Schelkun.

Printed in the United States of America on acid-free paper

10 9 8 7 6 5 4 3 2 1
First Edition

This book is dedicated to those devastated by the Memorial Day tornadoes and the Oregon District shootings, as well as the first responders who were so instrumental in the recovery, helping our community to remain Dayton Strong.

CONTENTS

1. I Told You So...9

2. Change...21

3. The Homecoming...31

4. Transition...39

5. Sticking to Principles...51

6. Moving in the Right Direction...........................61

7. A Difficult Summer...83

8. A Work in Progress...97

9. Wowing in Maui..107

10. This Team is For Real.....................................125

11. Exorcising Some Demons..............................139

12. A Missing Legend..151

13. Clutcher...165

14. Challenges Met..175

15. We Got the Dub...185

16. Surviving the Dog Days.................................195

17. What a Time to Be Alive................................207

18. And Then It Was Over....................................223

19. The Greatest Season......................................235

2019–2020 DAYTON FLYERS

OVERALL: 29–2
A-10: 18–0
HOME: 17–0
AWAY: 9–0
NEUTRAL: 3–2

PLAYERS

#0	Rodney Chatman	6'1", 178 lbs.	(RS) Junior	Lithonia, GA
#1	Obi Toppin	6'9", 220 lbs.	(RS) Sophomore	Brooklyn, NY
#2	Ibi Watson	6'5", 203 lbs.	(RS) Junior	Pickerington, OH
#3	Trey Landers	6'5", 221 lbs.	Senior	Dayton, OH
#4	Jarod Becker	6'4", 180 lbs.	Freshman	Milford, OH
#10	Jalen Crutcher	6'1", 175 lbs.	Junior	Memphis, TN
#11	Sean Loughran	6'3", 200 lbs.	Freshman	Pittsburgh, PA
#14	Moulaye Sissoko	6'9", 248 lbs.	Freshman	Bamako, Mali
#31	Jhery Matos	6'5", 195 (RS)	Jr.	Santo Domingo, DOM REP
#32	Jordy Tshimanga	6'11", 268 lbs.	(RS) Junior	Montreal, Quebec
#33	Ryan Mikesell	6'7", 217 lbs.	Grad	St. Henry, OH
#35	Dwayne Cohill	6'2", 180 lbs.	Sophomore	Cleveland, OH
#40	Chase Johnson	6'9", 219 lbs.	(RS) Sophomore	Ripley, WV
#51	Drew Swerlein	6'0", 175 lbs.	(RS) Freshman	Perrysburg, OH
#52	Camron Greer	5'7", 160 lbs.	Junior	Country Club Hills, IL
#53	Christian Wilson	6'1", 160 lbs.	(RS) Sophomore	Dayton, OH

STAFF

HEAD COACH	Anthony Grant
ASSOCIATE HEAD COACH	Anthony Solomon
ASSISTANT COACH	Ricardo Greer
ASSISTANT COACH	Darren Hertz
RECRUITING COORDINATOR	Andy Farrell
DIRECTOR OF PLAYER DEVELOPMENT	Brett Comer
DIR. OF BASKETBALL OPERATIONS	James Haring
GRADUATE ASSISTANT	Sean Damaska
GRADUATE ASSISTANT	Khyle Marshall
TRAINER	Mike Mulcahey
STRENGTH AND CONDITIONING	Casey Cathrall

STUDENT MANAGERS

Seniors	Alex Reilly
	Henry Stark
	Jack Walsh
Juniors	Matt Weckesser
	Alex Roberts
	Joe Geraghty
	Seth Jones
	Marin Reis
Sophomores	Pat Edwards
	John Miller
	Murphy Weiland
Freshmen	Ben Liptrap
	John Malkoski
	Chad Yohey

Trey Landers addresses the crowd

01

I TOLD YOU SO

I DIDN'T SAY IT ON THE AIR ON WHIO Radio that night, but I had on more than one occasion pointed out that when it came to the 2019–2020 Dayton Flyers basketball team, I was right, and a lot of people were wrong.

On October 24, 2019, the Atlantic Ten released the results of its preseason poll, as voted on by the coaches in the league and select members of the media. Defending champion VCU was an overwhelming pick to repeat, receiving 19 of a possible 28 first-place votes. Davidson was picked second and received 8 first-place votes. The Dayton Flyers were projected to finish third by the pollsters and received just one vote for first place. That vote belonged to me.

I told you so.

Was I an unmitigated biased homer, or did I possess some great basketball intellect, because on March 7, 2020, I was watching the Flyers cut down the nets at the UD Arena after completing a perfect 18–0 A-10 campaign with a 76–51 win over George Washington. I'd like to think it was a combination of the two factors that led me to put Dayton on the top line of my ballot.

I liked this team in that I liked the individuals. The players, coaches, and staff formed the highest character group I had been around—individually solid human beings for whom I wished only the best. But it was not my desire to see the Flyers succeed that influenced my vote, as much as the knowledge I had that the other voters did not.

I had watched practices the previous season. I saw the huge upside of Ibi Watson, Rodney Chatman, Jordy Tshimanga, and Chase Johnson, who were sitting out their transfer years, waiting and preparing for the opportunity to play. But I also saw them over the course of the summer and early fall, how well they meshed with the returning players. This was a group that enjoyed being around each other, and I enjoyed being around them. As much as I liked each one individually, I loved the sum total of them as a group.

I knew they were talented. I knew they had high basketball IQs and were very coachable. I knew they cared about each other on and off the court. I knew they had sufficient depth to play in the manner in which Coach Anthony Grant wanted and would be able to avoid the late-game fatigue issues that had plagued them the previous season. I knew they had what it takes to win the A-10.

I told you so.

However, I never imagined an 18–0 mark in league play. Every year Dr. Steve Levitt and I make a friendly wager of lunch as to who can come closest to picking the Flyers final record. I won this year, with a guess of 26–5 overall, 15–3 in the A-10 with league losses on the road at VCU, Saint Louis, and Rhode Island. Gladly, I was wrong, as Dayton ran the table in league play and were now celebrating in front of a sellout crowd at the UD Arena, the record 14th of the season. A crowd of Flyer Faithful—known in the past for leaving early—was still in the Arena when Coach Grant took the mic to address them.

"A long day for our guys. A lot of good things happened for our program today," he said. "For the City of Dayton, we're so grateful to ESPN bringing *GameDay* to Dayton, Ohio."

The Saturday show from 11:00 to noon, featuring Rece Davis, Jay Bilas, Seth Greenberg, and LaPhonso Ellis, was paying its first visit to Dayton. In fact, it was the first time it was held at a venue from which ESPN was not broadcasting the game that day. The ESPN broadcast that night was Duke vs. North Carolina. So how did the Flyers' regular season finale against a sub-500 George Washington team merit national attention?

Jay Bilas talked about the Flyers prior to the show. "I knew that Obi Toppin was going to have a break-out year, and I wrote about that in October, that he was the breakout star of the year," Bilas said. "But I first thought that Dayton was a Final Four contender in Maui. I watched them practice and play three games, and they were the best team there."

While Anthony Grant later that day expressed his appreciation for *College GameDay* coming to Dayton, Bilas felt it was ESPN that should be thankful. "I've known about the UD Arena since my days working A-10 broadcasts, and I was well aware of the passion and the knowledgeable fan base."

However, the draw was not the students in the Red Scare with their faces painted and their flight attendant uniforms, or the longtime season ticket holders in red sweater vests, or Pep Band Director Willie Morris in his light-up coat. ESPN was there because Obi Toppin was a player-of-the-year candidate, because Anthony Grant was a coach-of-the-year candidate, and because the Dayton Flyers were playing as well as any team in college basketball.

"It's an honor for us to be here," continued Bilas. "Dayton's really good and they have really good guys. It's not fake. They get along really well on-and-off the court, and you can feel it."

Seth Greenberg echoed Bilas's comments on the makeup of this Flyer squad. "I think what makes this team so special is their chemistry. They are so much more than Obi Toppin. They have respect for each other and know how to play the game. They have joy in each other's success, and that's what makes them special."

Add to that the right man to lead them, and the right man for a moment in the national spotlight, Coach Anthony Grant.

With the UD Arena being used for the Atlantic 10 Women's Championship, the *College GameDay* broadcast had to be shifted to the much smaller Frericks Center on campus. Doors opened at 9:30, with the line—consisting largely of students—allowed to start forming at 7:30.

Special Assistant to the Head Coach and Recruiting Coordinator Andy Farrell recalled that morning:

> Right when Coach got into the office, I asked him if he would like to hop in the golf cart and drive to interact with the people in line and the students. His eyes lit up and he said "absolutely." We got in (me, Coach, Ricardo, and A. J.) and Coach was

in the front seat with me driving. As we passed by the first group of students at the entrance of the Frericks Center, all Coach said was "WOW!" Then the students started to come to give Coach high-fives. We drove slowly as the students started rushing toward the golf cart. The line of students was easily 7–15 students in row together, extending all the way past the chapel. As we drove slowly, the students kept coming closer and closer and eventually, once we got to where the Olson Center was, Coach just decided to get out of the golf cart and get into the center of it with the students. The students started chanting "A-G. A-G. A-G" and he was giving high-fives to everyone and taking selfies. Then one student started chanting "SPEECH, SPEECH, SPEECH" and everyone followed. Finally, Coach got the crowd a little quiet and he spoke to the students. The students hung on every word, like he was delivering them a pre-game speech.

I contrast that scene to something I witnessed the previous season when Dayton had played at Auburn.

After trailing by 19 at the half, the Flyers had battled back hard—playing a future Final Four team—before losing 82–72. Tigers Coach Bruce Pearl took to the PA afterwards, thanking students for their support and wishing them well in their upcoming final exams, and praised Dayton for the effort. Then when it became time for the post-game TV interview, Pearl came over to the press row near where I was seated and asked students to stand behind him during the interview. As he was talking to the TV announcers, with his hand behind his back, he was motioning for the students to make more noise and be more demonstrative. When the camera was shut off, he berated a member of the sports information department.

"We've got to do better than that," Pearl said. "That was a missed opportunity. Find out who is in charge of the student section and tell them they need to bring it next time."

Now I am not saying Bruce Pearl is a bad guy. I like him, despite his many critics in the sports world. But his approach with the students was to create a marketing opportunity for the program.

Coach Grant's visit with the students was not a photo op. Andy Farrell continued:

> After a few minutes interacting, Coach got back into the golf cart and we drove around the back of the chapel. Coach said, "Let's surprise the people in the back of the line" who had no idea what was going on near the front of the line or near the Olson Center, since the line was past the chapel. We pulled around quietly and Coach, once again, got out of the golf cart. He walked toward the back of the line and yelled, "WHAT'S EVERYONE IN LINE FOR?" At that moment, the students in the back of the line turned around and started to get excited. Taking selfies, giving Coach high-fives, and

loving every minute of his energy. Coach gave them the same "pregame pep talk" as he did to the others and thanked them for their support and passion for the university and for our program.

The Frericks Center was packed for game day. The pep band and cheerleaders were there, along with the Flyer football team and fans of all ages.

Rece Davis addressed the crowd before going on the air. "It's moments like this that are special," he said. "When the crowd is engaged and you're showing your love for your team, your school, your program. You guys are awesome."

Through the next hour, Coach Grant was interviewed, the team came out, and Bilas did his 94-feet Q & A with Obi, just as he had done in Maui.

"What's your favorite food that Mom makes?"

"Definitely empanadas."

There was a rather contrived take-off on *The Bachelor*, whereby Davis, Bilas, Ellis, and Greenberg each gave a rose to a UD cheerleader who represented a bubble team in the projected NCAA tournament field. The crowd roared whenever Dayton was mentioned and booed at any discussion of other games on the slate that day.

The Flyer Faithful were "Flyer'd Up" but had to wait another seven hours until game time.

Emotions began to climb up the steep roller coaster hill again around 6:47 p.m. The scene had shifted to the UD Arena, and Senior Day Ceremonies had begun. Senior managers Jack Walsh, Alex Reilly, and Henry Stark were introduced and made the walk across the floor along with their families. Then Trey Landers was next, the roar from the crowd nearly

drowning out the PA announcement of his achieve-
ments as a Flyer. The decibel level never dropped as
Ryan Mikesell followed. There were hugs from Coach
Grant, tears were shed, and the Flyer Faithful show-
ered their love on the senior class of the 2019–2020
Flyers. After a morning-long buildup to game day, an
hour-long made-for-TV pep rally, and an emotional
Senior Day, it was now time to play basketball.

George Washington came into the game 12–18
overall, and 6–11 in the Atlantic 10. However, the
mismatch on paper was anything but that through the
first half. GW scored the first basket of the game. Obi
Toppin tied the game moments later on a dunk and
gave Dayton its first lead by making a free throw to
complete a three-point play. Back-and-forth it went,
with the Colonials opening up a 19–12 lead with 9:24
to go in the half. The Flyers recovered to regain the
lead and were up 24–22 at the under-four-minute media time-out. The sellout crowd was anxiously awaiting an explosion, but the rest of the half UD missed
its final six shots and only added two Obi free throws
for a 26–25 halftime lead.

I do not know what was said at halftime, and I
have not asked. As close as I am to the team—players, coaches, and staff—I have always respected the
privacy of the coach-to-players interaction within the
confines of the locker room. But knowing what I do
know, any advice, admonitions, or adjustments were
delivered calmly and evenly.

The second half began much as the first. GW took
the lead on a layup by Jamison Battle, and the teams
essentially traded baskets over the next few minutes.
The score was tied at 37 with 13:57 to play.

"Chatman kicks it out to Obi, handoff to Crutcher.
Crutcher lobbing to Obi. Catch and a flush!" I described to the listening audience.

Then as he had all season at moments like this, Jalen Crutcher got hot, scoring the next 10 points, including a pair of 3's.

Then Obi Toppin began adding to his season highlight reel.

"Obi takes the pass. Backing Battle down and dunks in his face! He just dunked in his face."

Toppin added another dunk off of his own steal, to complete a 16–0 run by the Flyers. But he saved his best dunk at the UD Arena for last.

"Loose ball picked up by Trey Landers. He fires ahead to Obi—OH, HE DID IT AGAIN! BETWEEN THE LEGS AND THE WINDMILL DUNK."

He replicated last season's dunk (only better) vs. Georgia Southern. That dunk, a handful of games into his freshman year, became a coaching moment, as Grant pulled him aside to talk about being aware of time and score, as well as not providing an opponent motivation. This time all Coach had was smiles.

George Washington never recovered, and the arrival of the anticipated explosion then led to a series of curtain calls. Dwayne Cohill came in for Jalen Crutcher. Jordy Tshimanga replaced Toppin. Cameron Greer came in for Trey Landers and then Christian Wilson for Ryan Mikesell. Each player received a bear hug from Coach Grant. Emotions still ran high: emotions of pure joy.

Final score: Dayton 76, George Washington 51. A perfect 18–0 A-10 season, a school-record 29 wins, and a school-record-tying 20 wins in a row.

Coach Grant continued his post-game address to the crowd. "Our guys were bound and determined today. It was a very emotional day with Senior Day and what we had going on. But they weren't going to be denied. We wanted to be sure that we made history here tonight in front of you. So, thank you, and Go Flyers!"

Then it was a chance for the seniors to speak. First came Trey Landers, thanking his family and then singling out one of his teammates. "Me and Jalen been through every type of season. I know we had a season 14–17, bro. And I wanted to tell you from the bottom of my heart, I appreciate you."

And then the rest of his teammates. "I want to thank you all from the bottom of my heart. For the blood, sweat, and tears you put into this game, not just for me, but for Ryan, this organization, these fans. Obviously, this is my last game here, but guys, we're not done yet."

Ryan Mikesell was next, also thanking his family and teammates. "Thank you, Flyer Nation. I came here five years ago, not knowing what to expect. It's been a journey, to say the least. Two years ago, I had to have two hip surgeries. I had just met Coach Grant. I didn't know how he was going to react to the news. As soon as I told him I need to get it done, he accepted the fact. He kept his patience and worked me the past two years. I am grateful to him and the whole staff. Once again, thanks Flyer Nation. Like Trey said, we're not done. Let's cut down some nets."

The Dayton Flyers were 2020 outright A-10 Champs, were heading to Brooklyn as the number one seed in the A-10 Championship, and were projected to be a number one seed in the NCAA Tournament. But in less than a week it was all gone—the Flyers' post-season dreams a casualty of the coronavirus pandemic that soon held the entire world in its grip.

However, this is not the story of what was NOT. This is the story of the greatest start-to-finish season in the rich history of Dayton basketball. It's the story of a late-blooming, under-recruited, under-the-radar boy who became a man and the Player of the Year in the nation. It's the story of the Coach of the Year in the nation. It's the story of teamwork, togetherness, and joy. It's a story of the whole being greater than the sum of the parts. And it's the story of a culture, built for the long run.

I told you so.

**Flyers at 2017 NCAA tournament
in Indianapolis**

02

CHANGE

THE MOST SUCCESSFUL SEASON IN
Dayton basketball history ended on March 7, 2020,
but the story began on March 25, 2017.

I was having lunch with my mom at the Wester-
ville Grille in suburban Columbus, near the retire-
ment community in which she lives. My dad passed
away in 2014, and I have tried to make the trip to see
her every week or so since she moved into Friendship
Village in 2016. As I had been busy traveling with the
Flyers—first to the A-10 tournament in Pittsburgh
and then to the NCAA Tournament in Indianapolis—we had some catching up to do, so I ignored the
constant buzzing from my pocket. I make it a point
not to look at my phone when I am in a restaurant,
and especially when eating with my mom, who is not
a fan of modern communication devices.

However, the notification of incoming text messages was persistent, so I took a peek:

"Well, that sucks."

"What a way to ruin a Saturday."

"This is the worst news possible."

"Please tell me this isn't true."

I excused myself from the table, went to the restroom, and a quick look at my email explained why so many of my friends were upset.

Archie Miller was leaving Dayton to become the head coach at Indiana.

Archie had replaced Brian Gregory at UD in the spring of 2011, after BG left for Georgia Tech. It was Miller's first head coaching job, having been an assistant at Western Kentucky, North Carolina State, Ohio State, Arizona State, and most recently with his brother Sean at Arizona.

Inheriting a solid senior class that included Chris Johnson, Paul Williams, Luke Fabrizius, and Josh Parker, the Flyers' cupboard was not bare. Josh Benson was coming off of a knee injury the previous year, and Kevin Dillard was ready for action after sitting out following his transfer from Southern Illinois. Dayton won the opener over Western Illinois, stubbed its toe at Miami in a 72–67 overtime loss, and then went to Orlando and won the Old Spice Classic with victories over Wake Forest, Fairfield, and Minnesota, only to return home and get drubbed at home by Buffalo, 84–55. An equally lackluster performance at Murray State, and the Flyers were 5–3 heading to Alabama.

Anthony Grant was coaching the Crimson Tide, and Dan Hipsher, who had recruited him to come to Dayton as a player, was one of his assistants. The night before the game, Hipsher took my broadcast partner, Bucky Bockhorn, and me on a tour of the campus. The fraternity houses looked like plantations out of *Gone with the Wind*. The sorority houses surrounded Bryant-Denny Stadium, and Hip said on football game days the girls were decked out in dresses and heels—a far cry from the hoodies and Uggs seen on most campuses.

All of the athletic facilities were amazing. Each sport had its own playing venue, with one exception. Men's basketball shared an arena with women's gymnastics, and the gymnasts drew more fans for their meets than attend Tide basketball games.

Alabama came into the game ranked 16th in the nation, but behind 20 points from Chris Johnson and 14 points and a solid floor game from Kevin Dillard (who former Tide coach and TV analyst Wimp Sanderson called a "Booger Bear"), Dayton won 74–62. The Flyers won four of the next five, including a win over another SEC team, Ole Miss, and after beating Saint Louis and Temple to start the A-10 season, optimism was high. But Dayton was 7–7 the rest of the year and exited the NIT quietly with a first-round loss at Iowa.

Archie's second year saw the string of 20-plus wins and post-season appearances come to an end. The Flyers were 17–14, losing to Butler in the first round of the A-10 tournament. A CBI bid was on the table. Miller asked the two seniors, Dillard and Benson, if they wanted to play. They said if the rest of the guys did, sure. It was a tepid enough response to just pack things up for next year.

The 2013–14 season was detailed in my previous book, *True Team: The Dayton Flyers' Run to the Elite Eight.* A strong showing in Maui, an up-and-down December, a horrific start to the A-10 season in January, then winning 9 out of 10 to end the regular season, which set the stage for the tourney run that lives forever in the hearts and minds of Flyer fans.

Vee Sanford's game-winning shot takes down Ohio State, Dyshawn Pierre's clutch free throws and a deep three late by Jordan Sibert provide the upset win over

Syracuse, a complete team effort beat Stanford 82–72 in a game that was not really that close, before bowing out to Florida.

Sanford, Devin Oliver, and Matt Kavanaugh were the seniors on that team, and a trio of freshmen— Scoochie Smith, Kyle Davis, and Kendall Pollard— collectively averaged 7.6 points a game. Together, they became the foundation of a string of successful years.

Dayton ran into adversity the following season, 2014–15. After starting the season 7–1, the Flyers lost at Arkansas. Upon returning to campus that night, Devon Scott and Jalen Robinson went into a residence hall and stole items from dorm rooms. They were dismissed from the team. Ryan Bass, a Dayton native and grad transfer from Oakland, suffered a season-ending concussion. Junior college transfer Detwon Rogers initially battled a knee issue and then some academic issues and never appeared in a game. With only six scholarship players plus walk-on Bobby Wehrli, who was given a scholarship the second semester, Dayton managed to win 25 games, falling to VCU in the A-10 Finals.

On Selection Sunday, the travel party went to a restaurant in Yonkers, New York, owned by a UD grad, to see where the Flyers would be playing in the NCAA Tournament. As CBS unveiled the bracket, they said, "Providence, seeded 6th in the East, will play the winner of the Boise State vs. Dayton game in the First Four," so quickly everyone in the room was either stunned or simply didn't hear it clearly.

While administrators were scrambling to put together a plan for tickets, Archie and his staff huddled up on the flight back. Once the team arrived back on campus, Archie took them into a meeting room, they re-watched the selection show, and they jumped up and down and celebrated when Dayton was announced.

That First Four game vs. Boise State in March 2015 was the loudest I had ever experienced in the UD Arena, the crescendo pitch coming when Jordan Sibert hit the go-ahead shot and then Kyle Davis sealed the victory with a defensive stop. It was Sibert's last game on that floor. He had hit a game-winning shot in his first game, vs. IUPU Fort Wayne in 2013, and repeated the feat in his final game.

Bags were packed and I rode the bus over to Columbus with the team for the matchup with Providence, which the Flyers won in front of an overwhelmingly pro-UD crowd. In the round of 32, the Magnificent 7, a nickname given to this undermanned group of Flyers, finally ran out of gas and were eliminated by Oklahoma.

The next season (2015–16) produced 25 wins and a share of the A-10 title. With Scoochie, Kendall, and Kyle as the core, they were joined by James Madison transfer Charles Cooke and redshirt freshman Steve McElvene. Cooke led the team in scoring at 15.5 points a game, and McElvene, with a personality as big as his 6'11" frame, became an instant crowd favorite, setting a school record with 55 blocked shots, prompting the Red Scare to hold up signs saying, "Steve Says No" whenever he swatted one away.

The Flyers were blown out by Syracuse 70–51 in the field of 64, but you could tell Big Steve was starting to really come into his own. His future, and the future for the Flyers, who only lost seniors Dyshawn Pierre and Bobby Wehrli, was bright.

That all came to a shocking end when McElvene collapsed and died at his home in Fort Wayne on May 12. It was the second time in my career that a Flyer player had suddenly passed away, evoking the painful memories of Chris Daniels's death in 1996. I didn't get to go to his funeral in Indiana, as it was the same day as my daughter Andrea's graduation from high school. I never got to say a proper goodbye to Big Steve, and like his teammates, coaches, and Flyer Fans, I am still haunted with thoughts of "what if."

Josh Cunningham was eligible the next season (2016–17) after sitting out his transfer year from Bradley. He was to fill the void in the middle, not as a shot blocker, but scoring and rebounding, but he went down with an ankle injury in a win at Alabama in the second game of the season. Once again, the Flyers overcame adversity to not only get back to the NCAA Tournament, but winning the A-10 title outright, beating VCU at the Arena in overtime.

When they lost to Wichita State in the NCAA Tournament in Indianapolis on March 17, 2017, Scooch, Kyle, and Kendall had played in four straight NCAA Tournaments—something no Dayton team had ever done. Their 102 wins were the most by any class in school history, eclipsing the previous mark of 94 set by the seniors on the 2010 NIT Championship team.

Despite two quick one-game-and-out exits from the NCAA Tournament in 2016 and '17 and the departure of that record-setting group of seniors, Dayton fans felt optimistic that the string of success would continue. However, Dayton fans also felt that success was directly linked to Archie Miller remaining.

The Flyers were in Indianapolis preparing to meet Wichita State in the NCAA Tournament. Before the open practice at Bankers Life Fieldhouse, Dayton practiced at the University of Indianapolis (not to be confused with IUPUI). It was during practice that word got out that Tom Crean had been fired at Indiana. No one seemed too surprised, and the practice went on with the focus on putting together a game plan vs. the Shockers.

On the bus ride back downtown, I sat with Archie's dad, John. He asked me what I knew about Crean and why he was fired. I told him I had heard that despite a decent record, Crean was rubbing some people in Hoosier Land the wrong way. I speculated not making the tournament may have been an excuse for his firing, as opposed to a reason.

Part of the public practices at an NCAA tournament venue is a press conference before or after involving the head coach and select players. Archie Miller walked into the interview room in Indianapolis, just hours after Tom Crean had been fired as the head basketball coach at Indiana University. I may have been the only person who directed a question to Archie about the Flyers or the matchup with the Shockers. National media, and the TV, radio, and newspaper reporters from Indianapolis all peppered him with questions as to his interest in the IU job. Archie deflected every single one, saying his focus was on the task at hand.

In retrospect, and based upon my relationship with Archie through the years, I believe he was completely honest with reporters that day. Archie Miller may be the most singularly focused individual I have ever known. He truly concentrated on one thing and one thing only, and that was how to beat Wichita State.

The Shockers were everyone's favorite upset pick as a 10 seed against the 7th-seeded Flyers, and even though Dayton led by two at the half, I could sense they were in trouble. The second half was a back-and-forth battle, with Wichita State taking the lead for good at about the 7-minute mark and pulling away for a 64–58 win. Scoochie Smith was magnificent, scoring 25 points.

"You tell me that's not an NBA player!" Archie said afterward on his post-game radio interview with me.

However, Scooch did not get a lot of help. Charles

Cooke was 1-for-10 from the field and finished with just 6 points. Xeyrius Williams was 1-for-9 and had just 3 points.

The bus ride back to Dayton was relatively quiet, with Archie spending most of it on the phone to Kentucky Coach John Calipari about what the Cats needed to do to beat Wichita State the next day. Calipari grew up in the same town as Archie and was a close friend of the Miller family.

One week later my phone blew up during my lunch in Columbus.

When I got back to Dayton, I texted Archie to congratulate him and wish him well. Immediately, my phone rang.

"How are you doing?" he asked.

"I'm sad," I answered.

He replied. "I'm sad too, and I think you can understand why. You and Bucky were my best friends in Dayton."

I was taken aback. I considered Archie a friend, but outside of the basketball season, we never really interacted socially. But then again, Archie did not socialize much, if at all. Like I said, singularly focused. He didn't play golf, tennis, or fish. Outside of basketball and his family, he had no interests except for the Pittsburgh Steelers. He shared that passion with Bucky, so I can see why we were his Dayton friends. We remain friends and keep in touch via email and texts. It upsets me that some Flyer Faithful hold a grudge against Archie. During the game day broadcast, there were boos every time Indiana was mentioned. Archie advanced the program and even though he is no longer here, I firmly believe UD will always hold a special place in his heart. The first text I received after the Flyers' overtime loss to Kansas in the Maui Invitational was from him. "Man, that was close. I thought we had them."

Later on that Saturday in 2017, University of Dayton Director of Athletics Neil Sullivan met with reporters. "We like Archie and we're glad he was our coach for the last six years," he said. "Certainly, sad to see him go, but we are prepared to move forward."

When Brian Gregory left for Georgia Tech, part of his exit entailed a home-and-home series between the Flyers and Yellow Jackets. Sullivan told reporters that there was no requirement for Archie and Indiana to play Dayton. Neil did not elaborate. I speculate that within Archie's contract with UD there were two to three "out" schools included, whereby he could leave without having to be bought out or required to play a series with Dayton.

Some of the media members wondered if Miller left for greener pastures, as in financially greener. Sullivan said money was not the issue. "Ultimately, Coach Miller had to make a decision for his future and his best interest. But I can assure everybody that it was a very aggressive pursuit on our behalf for him to remain our coach."

As shocking and surreal as that day felt, however, it did not come as a surprise. Not to fans, not to me, not to Neil Sullivan. "It's no secret that Archie has been a highly sought-after coach. I think it's a testament to what we do here, a testament to him, not only him. It's a testament to our University, our fan base, and the resources we provide to be successful."

Sullivan said he would head up the process of searching for the next Flyers coach with help from former AD Tim Wabler and Associate Athletic Directors Robby Poteat and Adam Tschuor. "We'll be deliberate, we'll be intentional, and we'll be methodical to make sure we have someone who represents this University in the right way."

In less than a week they found that man.

Anthony Grant and Larry

03

THE HOMECOMING

DAN HIPSHER JOINED DON DONOHER'S staff at the University of Dayton in 1980. After graduating from Bowling Green State University in 1977 after a playing career in which he was a two-time captain, he spent a year at Miami University in Oxford, Ohio, as a grad assistant and then a year at Miami-Dade Community College in Florida as an assistant coach. It was there he met Shakey Rodriguez, the former legendary head coach at Miami Senior High School.

In the fall of 1982 Rodriguez let Hipsher know that he had a player that might be a good fit for the Flyers, seventeen-year-old Anthony Grant. After checking him out, he sent Coach Donoher to Florida to meet with the family. "I tell you, Larry, almost from the very first time I went into that home and met his parents, I knew here was a special kid," Donoher told me, thirty-four years later. "The father had a body like Anthony, tough construction worker. Had about a fourth-grade education. He grilled me about the lifestyle at the University of Dayton, and how did we take care of the kids and how did we prepare them."

Donoher met with the approval of the Grant family, most of the year . . . "This is the only problem we ever had with Anthony," Donoher said. "The mom, she had no eyes for Christmas night practices. We would turn 'em loose for a few days, but we had no other choice but to practice Christmas night. And we used to sweat it out. 'Is Grant going to be back for practice or not?' because she thought that was barbaric."

My first conversation with Anthony Grant came shortly after that meeting. I was in my first year of broadcasting Flyer games on WHIO, and Hipsher gave me Anthony's number. I called him up and recorded a phone interview in which he announced his intent to play college basketball at the University of Dayton.

I broadcast every game of Grant's UD playing career, which wasn't much his freshman year. He played with Roosevelt Chapman, Dayton's all-time leading scorer and appeared in 18 games, averaging 1 point per game. Dan Christie was a fellow freshman on that team and remembers meeting Anthony shortly after they both arrived on campus.

"We go down to the PAC and shoot around a little bit. All of a sudden, he barely jumps and dunks it behind his back. Not many guys like that from Oak Harbor, Ohio."

Despite his athleticism, he was not going to take any minutes away from Chapman. "The fact that Chap went for 51 against him in the very first scrimmage we had as a freshman didn't indicate he was going to get a lot of playing time that year, but the next three years . . . always working, always the last guy to leave the gym, just tremendous human being. He was always a team guy, never copped an attitude, always pushing other people to be better," Christie remembered.

Grant became a starter for those three years and a team captain his senior year. His career numbers were solid, but not stellar: 11.6 points and 6.7 rebounds per game.

On April 1, 2017, Don Donoher, Dan Christie, and other former Flyers, including Capital University Coach Damon Goodwin, were gathered in the UD Arena Flight Deck to welcome Anthony Grant back home.

University of Dayton President Dr. Eric Spina was the first to speak. "Exactly one week ago some people were asking if the sun would come up again. It has, seven times, and today the sun is shining brighter than ever."

I had learned that Grant was the pick on Thursday of that week, and soon the news broke throughout Flyer Nation. There was no drama as Neil Sullivan took the podium next. "The best I can describe him, he's a proven winner. He has won basketball games at the highest level. He's coached at the highest level and he's played at the highest level," Sullivan began.

After his playing career ended at UD, Grant had spent the summer playing for the Miami Tropics in the short-lived United States Basketball League. He got into coaching, first as an assistant to Shakey Rodriguez at his alma mater, Miami Senior. In 1993 Dan Hipsher asked him to join his staff at Stetson. When Don Donoher was fired by Dayton in 1989, Hipsher had been the head coach at Wittenberg for four years before taking over at Stetson. After one year at Stetson, Grant was hired by Billy Donovan at Marshall, and he followed him to Florida two years later, where he was part of a staff that won the National Championship in 2006. The Gators repeated in 2007 with many players Grant had recruited and developed, but by then he had his first collegiate head coaching opportunity at VCU. He won 28 games his first year, advancing to the second round of the NCAA Tournament with an upset of Duke, went to the NIT the following year, and back to the NCAA in 2009. After that, he spent six years at Alabama, where he was 117–85 with one trip to the NCAA Tournament and two to the NIT. He was fired after going 18–14 in the 2014–2015 season, and then reunited with Billy Donavan, this time in the NBA on Donavan's staff with the Oklahoma City Thunder, working with players such as Kevin Durant and Russell Westbrook.

"I followed him when he was at Alabama. He cracked the whip on some unruly individuals down there, and a lot of coaches would have looked the other way and let it go on. He won't let anything go on. He's just as interested in their development as people—and whatever the rules are, he's going to enforce them. And no one is going to skate. He'll do it the right way, and that's been the Dayton tradition," Donoher told me that day.

Although Neil Sullivan was not around Dayton during Grant's playing days, he was very familiar with Anthony Grant the coach. "I followed his career. I think I had every piece of information on him, a complete file on his recruits, stats, analytics," Sullivan told me. "As an athletic director, you always have that proverbial 'list.'"

There was no shortage of people who wanted to be the next coach of the Flyers. "The number of people interested in the job, I couldn't begin to count. The amount of phone calls and texts I received from assistant coaches, former head coaches, sitting head coaches speaking on behalf of assistants, and agents was in the hundreds in the first twelve hours," Sullivan continued. "ADs employ search firms, I think, to act as a triage of all that information."

It was Sullivan who initiated contact with Grant, beginning with a phone call, and then another. "We had a good conversation one morning, and I called him back an hour later. He was in Orlando for a game between the Thunder and the Magic. I told him I would be there by three in the afternoon and I had a hotel suite reserved for us to meet. We had a four-hour, sit-down discussion."

Sullivan left that meeting, ready to make an offer. "His completeness, his professionalism, and the totality of our conversation made me have a pretty good feeling as I was flying back that I had the guy. What impressed me most was something he said that no other coach I had ever interviewed said. Most, if not all, candidates talk about themselves, sell themselves, but he was pushing for the University of Dayton. He felt he was the right candidate for the job, but if not, he really cared that we made the right hire. He took things up a level with that."

Now he was introducing the most important hire to date in his athletic administrative career, referencing the conversations he had with Grant about his vision for Flyer basketball. "He talked about long-term success, about how bad he wants to be here, and how bad he wants to succeed not just in the short term but the long term, which was very important to us. Not just players leaving with a degree, but a meaningful degree—better people than when they came in. We talked about winning A-10 championships, and instead of winning he used the term *dominating* to win A-10 championships."

How prophetic do those words ring after an 18–0 run to the 2020 title!

Then it was Anthony Grant's chance to say his first public words as the coach of his alma mater. "Thirty-four years ago, I came here for a visit to see a game [vs. DePaul, an 80–71 UD win], to see if this would be a place to fit me as a student athlete. The crowd was amazing. It sold me right there. This is where I want to come, if I could fool these guys into giving me a scholarship."

Grant, the former player, now addressed his comments to the current Flyer players. "This is a special place. This is, to me, a labor of love. I'm in it for you. Today, they say, it's about me. This is probably the most you'll hear me talk about myself. This program is about the community, the city of Dayton. It's about you guys."

He then spoke about style of play, something the players were obviously interested in, but of interest as well to fans. "On offense, we're going to be attacking, we're going to be unselfish and we're going to be efficient," he continued. "On defense, aggressive, disruptive, disciplined."

Again, prophetic words, when you look at the 2019–2020 season. Three years after presenting that vision, the Flyers led the nation in field goal percentage (52.5%), were second in the nation in offensive efficiency (1.14 points per possession), and third in the nation in assists per game (17.6).

When the press conference wrapped up, Coach Grant joined me live on radio and talked about the whirlwind week. Just seven days prior, he had no idea he would be coming back to Dayton. "Honestly, I never thought the opportunity for me would come up. This happened really fast. I think I heard the news as we were boarding for a three-game road trip to go to

Houston. After the Houston game we were in Dallas, and I got the phone call from Neil saying they wanted to talk."

He talked about the coaching influences in his life, beginning with Shakey Rodriguez, his high school coach for whom he later worked as an assistant and was the best man at his wedding. "Coach Donoher installed in me confidence and attention to detail. He took me from a boy to a man. Billy Donavan is like a family member, having spent fourteen years of my coaching career working with or for him. He's the best. A Hall-of-Famer."

I had seen firsthand what Anthony Grant's work ethic was like as a player and, like Dan Christie said, he was a team guy. I wondered how a "we" guy coaches the "me" generation of players. He responded, "They want to know that you care about them, that you have their best interest at heart, and at the end of the day they can be successful accomplishing their goals and dreams. Back in the day when I played it was, "I want you to run through that wall." "OK, I'm gonna run through that wall." Now you tell a kid to run through that wall, they want to know why. If they believe in what you are doing, they're going to run through that wall."

The 2019–2020 Dayton Flyers ran through walls and often flew over top of them! The most successful season in UD history came in just the third year of the Anthony Grant era. From a distance, that would appear to be an instant success, but it was a gradual and at times painful process.

It began with a homecoming.

Larry and Brooks Hall

04

TRANSITION

BEFORE PRACTICE BEGAN IN THE FALL
of 2017, before there were any balls bouncing in the
gym, Grant began to build a team that fit his vision
for Dayton basketball.

"Right after he was hired, instead of giving the
guys a workout routine, he told them he was going
to be busy hiring a staff and recruiting, and it was up
to them to take care of things in the classroom, doing
the right things," remembered Neil Sullivan. "Academic Advisor Beth Flach said to me, 'Did he really
just prioritize academics?!'"

Over the past three years, Flach says that priority
did not change:

> Coach Grant is in a unique position
> as the leader of the team because he
> is also an alum. He cares about the
> experience of the student-athletes

from a holistic perspective because he was once in their shoes. He also knows the value of the education he received while at UD, and he has a desire to instill those same values as a part of his mission as the head coach. Working with Coach Grant and his entire staff is rewarding for me on a daily basis because they care . . . very simply put, they care about their student-athletes and they care about those of us who work with them. My experience is valued, I am listened to, and I have an equal seat at the table with the resources needed to help each student meet their academic goals. It's beyond cool to have a professor say to me, "I once taught Anthony, and now I have one of his students in my class." That history is exceptional to be a part of.

It wasn't just lip service. In his first few weeks on the job, a player skipped a class. Grant brought the whole team in to run early in the morning. A message was delivered.

While leaving the players to focus on their academics, Grant began the process of visiting the incoming recruits and hiring a staff.

The first to be hired was Darren Hertz, as Assistant to the Head Coach. He came to Dayton after one year at Illinois, having spent the previous nineteen years at Florida. Hertz was an All-Dade County point guard his senior year at Miami Killian High School.

"It was the spring of 1996. The staff had just come to Florida from Marshall," Hertz told me. "I was trying to get my foot in the door and had met with Lon Kruger a month earlier and was going to be working camp. Kruger went to Illinois and I thought I had lost my 'in.' My dad knew Shakey Rodriguez [Anthony's HS coach] and that was my connection."

Hertz became a student assistant with the Gators, then video coordinator, Assistant to the Head Coach, and Director of Basketball Operations. Ten of those years in Gainesville, he was on the same staff with Anthony Grant.

James Kane became the second staff member to reunite with Grant. Kane had spent six years at Murray State after working for Grant, first at VCU and then at Alabama. He actually met Anthony while he was a student at Florida. He and two other students beat Grant and two other members of the Gator staff in a game of three-on-three, with the prize for the students being the chance to accompany the team on a charter flight to a game. Kane only spent one year at Dayton but made a lasting impact with his recruitment of Jalen Crutcher.

Ricardo Greer was driving to the Final Four. "Donnie Jones called me and said he had a good friend who is the new head coach at Dayton."

Donnie Jones had worked with Anthony Grant as part of Billy Donovan's staff, first at Marshall and then at Florida. Jones then went back to Marshall as the head coach from 2007–2010 before taking the job at Central Florida. He was let go in March of 2016. Ricardo Greer grew up in the Washington Heights neighborhood of New York City. His parents were both natives of the Dominican Republic.

"I was born in the US, "Greer told me. "Then we moved to the Dominican Republic and I lived there until I was three before we moved back to New York."

Greer would return to the DR to visit family, and

then as a high school player, became a member of the under-20 national team. Then when he was a junior at the University of Pittsburgh, he became a member of the Dominican Republic National Team, competing in the Pan American Games and in his final year on the squad in 2009, captaining the team that qualified for the World Championships.

His Dominican career not only coincided with his collegiate career at Pitt, where he was a two-time All-Big East selection, but also his European career, the bulk of it spent in France. He was a five-time French Pro-League All-Star, League MVP in 2010, and this past spring was inducted into the French Basketball Hall of Fame.

His playing background, both at Pitt and overseas, serves him well as a recruiter and coach.

"All kids want to play pro basketball, whether it's the NBA or abroad," he said. "I am a carbon copy of what they want to be. I can talk to them about the grind and the work it takes. I can help them get to where they want to be."

He was familiar with the University of Dayton before joining Anthony Grant, having played AAU ball with former Flyer assistant Allen Griffin and against former UD player Tony Stanley in high school and in France. "My second pro game in France, Tony and I had dinner the night before. I went out and scored 30 points the next day."

When Anthony Solomon was named Associate Head Coach it marked his second stint with Dayton basketball. Solomon was on Brian Gregory's staff in the 2007–2008 season, before leaving to return to Notre Dame, where he had been an assistant before taking over a troubled St. Bonaventure program in 2003. The Bonnies were coming off the "welding certificate" scandal. Jan van Breda Kolff was fired, the athletic director resigned, and school president Robert Wickenheiser stepped down after acknowledging he approved the transfer of a player who had only a welding certificate from a community college in Georgia. St. Bonaventure was banned from the A-10 tournament and forfeited their last regular season game, which was to have been against the Dayton Flyers.

Solomon cleaned up the program but saw little success on the court. One coup, however, was the recruitment of Michael Lee, luring the slender 6'7" forward to leave West Palm Beach, Florida, for the frozen tundra of Olean, New York. "I had seen him on film and heard some good things about him, so I flew down to Florida," he later told me. "My plane was delayed and I arrived at the gym late, walking in carrying my suitcase. Practice had ended and he already had one shoe off. I asked the coach if he could have him come back on the court since I had come all that way to see him. I had him take the ball from the right block, one dribble and hook shot. Lefty. Looked like Sam Perkins. Then from the middle, spin move to the basket. Finally, from the free throw line step into a jump shot. Swish. Sam Perkins. I told the coach, 'I'll take him. I've seen enough.'"

It was one thing to want Lee to come to St. Bonaventure, it was a larger challenge for Solomon to get Lee to commit. "He came on his visit and it was snowing bad, but he was sleeping in the car. About fifteen minutes from campus he woke up and said, 'I've never seen snow like that!' I told him he would be too busy playing so many minutes he wouldn't know what the weather was like."

Lee turned into a nice player for the Bonnies and was their leading scorer in Solomon's final year, when he was fired after a 7–22 season.

The "glue" hire in that spring may have been to

bring Andy Farrell back to UD as the Director of Player Development.

Since 2003, with the exception of one year, there has been a Farrell brother on staff at the University of Dayton. It began in 2003 when Andy Farrell became a student manager.

"I had some Division III offers coming out of Carroll High School, "said Andy. "But my dream was to walk on at UD."

Forty-five players showed up for walk-on tryouts in the fall of 2003, Brian Gregory's first year as Dayton's head coach. At the end of the tryout, Gregory approached Andy.

"He told me, 'You are not making the team, but I can see in your eyes that you love the game. I want you to be a student manager.'"

Andy took the weekend to think it over, and then accepted, spending his four undergrad years at Dayton doing a lot of thankless jobs while learning the game from a non-player standpoint. His senior year, his older brother, Matt, joined the team as a graduate assistant and became the Director of Basketball Operations in August of 2007, a position he held through the end of the 2010–2011 season.

After Andy left UD, his twin brother, Eric, came on board as a graduate assistant. And when Archie Miller arrived in the spring of 2011, Eric became Assistant Director of Basketball Operations. He left that job at the end of the 2015–2016 season to work for the First Four committee. That following year was the only year without a Farrell since 2003, as Andy returned to Dayton as Director of Scouting and Program Development.

His return marked a reunion with Anthony Grant, for whom he worked as a graduate assistant at VCU before joining Oliver Purnell for two years at Clemson and two years at DePaul. After a brief stop at Longwood University in Virginia, Andy spent three seasons at Southwest Mississippi Community College and then got the call from Grant. "I believe in him and everything he stands for. At every stop in my career I have always consulted him, Brian Gregory, and Billy Schmidt [former Gregory assistant] before taking a new job."

The Farrell brothers' love affair with Flyer basketball began almost at birth. Twins Andy and Eric attended their first game when they were four months old and they later worked as ball boys. "I have a picture of us and Josh Postorino," laughed Andy.

All three brothers played on, and later coached, Salvation Army teams. Eric and Andy played four years at Carroll. Matt played freshman ball and then later was the freshman coach as a senior. Eric was an assistant high school coach at Troy and Springboro. With Eric working for the Dayton Area Homebuilder's Association and Matt with Tangram Flex, a software re-engineering firm, Andy is the only Farrell brother still in coaching. He says his background gives him a unique role on Anthony Grant's staff.

"As the only coach born and raised in Ohio, I have been able to build meaningful relationships with high school and AAU coaches. I have kept in touch through the years, and now I can connect our staff to the right people."

Another key to a smooth transition was the retention of Athletic Trainer Mike Mulcahey, who joined the Sports Medicine staff at UD in 2014. He told me he gave no consideration whatsoever to leaving after Archie Miller's departure. His role would prove to be critical in the next two seasons, in rehabbing Ryan Mikesell from double hip surgery, the physical development of Obi Toppin, and helping manage the physical load of what would prove to be a short bench.

Casey Cathrall was hired by Grant to be the Strength and Conditioning Coach, coming to Dayton from Louisiana Tech, having previously worked at University of Maryland-Baltimore County and Florida International University.

Ten returning players, including walk-ons Joey Gruden and Jack Westerfield, were in the first meeting with the Flyers new coach. Four recruits had been signed for the upcoming season. There was a time in college basketball when those numbers would remain unchanged, despite a coaching change, but not in the current landscape.

Of the five incoming freshman, three—Matej Svoboda, Jordan Pierce, and Jordan Davis—opted to stay Flyers. Nahziah Carter reopened his recruitment and signed with Washington. He started 31 of 32 games for the Huskies last season and averaged 12.2 points per game. McKinley Wright, who seemed the heir apparent to Scoochie Smith at point guard, also was released from his letter of intent. He signed with Colorado and has been a star for the Buffaloes. He was freshman of the year in the Pac-12 and first team all-conference the next two seasons.

Shortly after Grant arrived, rising junior Ryan Mikesell was diagnosed with impingement in both hips and would require surgery. It had affected his play that season.

"I told Archie to take me out of the game a couple of times," he told me. "I couldn't move well enough to defend. I was a liability."

Mikesell had the first surgery on April 16, 2017, and the second in June. The prognosis for recovery was at least six months, which would mean he wouldn't be able to play until December at the earliest.

"We'll determine from there once we see how he progresses what the next step will be," Grant told David Jablonski of the *Dayton Daily News*. "I think it would be premature to say one way or the other in terms of his status for next season. That's all we know right now."

Later in the summer another rising junior, Sam Miller, got into an altercation at a bar in Beavercreek and was arrested. Embarrassing video from the jail became public, and in August he was suspended from the University of Dayton for the first semester, his basketball scholarship revoked for the year. He subsequently transferred to the College of Charleston, where he averaged 8.4 points and 5.9 rebounds a game in the 2019–2020 season.

The first recruit of the Anthony Grant era was Jalen Crutcher on May 6, 2017. Crutcher had de-committed from Chattanooga, where he had signed to play for Coach Matt McCall who left to take the job at UMass. Ironically, McCall and Grant are close friends, stemming from their days on the Billy Donavan staff at Florida. Flyer Assistant James Kane had recruited Crutcher, when he was at Murray State, and Scoochie Smith helped seal the deal, spending time with Crutcher who made his visit to Dayton on Scooch's graduation weekend.

A few weeks after, the "Peanut Butter" (Crutcher) of the Peanut Butter and Jam duo signed, "Jam" (Toppin) became a Flyer.

The 2020 National Player of the Year received no Division I offers as a 6'5" senior at Ossining High School in New York. Obi Toppin was set to go to a junior college when his godfather, Victor Monaros, who had played college basketball at Florida A&M, was able to get him a scholarship to Mt. Zion Prep in Baltimore. Monaros also was acquainted with Flyer

Assistant Coach Ricardo Greer.

"I told AG that I have a friend who has a guy we need. I knew Victor Monaros from playing on the Dominican National Team. When I was at UCF, I was recruiting Obi. I was trying to get him to come there when I got the job at Dayton," recalled Greer.

By the time Dayton showed interest, Obi had grown to 6'8" during his prep year. When he flew in for his official visit, he thought he was going to Daytona, Florida!

"Yes, I thought I was going to Daytona, because I really didn't know that much about Dayton, but once I got on the plane, I knew it was for me. Everyone on the plane knew who I was and said they wanted me to come be a Flyer."

Obi's mom, Roni Toppin, was impressed after going on three previous visits to schools. "Everyone was so friendly," she recalled. "I really didn't know anything about Dayton, but when we landed, a woman who was on the plane saw how tall Obi was and asked if he was coming to UD. The whole visit was so welcoming and it was a beautiful campus."

He signed with UD in May of 2017, but in September he was declared ineligible by the NCAA Clearinghouse and would have to sit out the 2017–2018 season as an academic redshirt.

While Obi was sitting out, he would still be allowed to practice with the team the full season. That had not been the case for Kostas Antetokounmpo (who will remain simply Kostas hereafter to give my spell-check a break). The younger brother of Giannis, the star of the Milwaukee Bucks and eventual NBA MVP, had only been able to practice the second semester of the previous season. Athletic and 6'10", though thin and borderline frail, Kostas had a lot of untapped potential.

Here is what the roster of available players looked like when the Flyers got ready to practice in the fall of 2017:

> *SENIORS*
> Darrell Davis
> Joey Gruden (walk-on)
> *JUNIORS*
> Josh Cunningham
> Xeyrius Williams
> John Crosby
> Jack Westerfield (walk-on)
> *SOPHOMORES*
> Trey Landers
> *FRESHMAN*
> Jalen Crutcher
> Jordan Davis
> Kostas Antetokounmpo
> Matej Svoboda
> Jordan Pierce
> Cameron Greer (walk-on)
> Dalton Stewart (walk-on)

The roster was set. The staff was hired. It was time for the Anthony Grant era to begin.

Josh Cunningham

05

STICKING TO PRINCIPLES

IN HIS FIRST GAME COACHING FROM the home bench at the UD Arena, Anthony Grant saw his Flyers post a 79–61 exhibition win over Ohio Dominican. The five returning healthy scholarship players started: Senior Darrell Davis, Juniors Josh Cunningham, John Crosby, and Xeyrius Williams, and sophomore Trey Landers. Cunningham led the way with 22 points, with Darrell Davis adding 14 and newcomer Matej Svoboda off the bench with 13. Of the freshmen, Jalen Crutcher logged the most minutes with 6 points and 4 assists in 23 minutes.

Afterward I talked to Coach Grant. "I thought our guys were able to sustain effort, for the most part, for 40 minutes tonight. I thought we did a really good job of rebounding the basketball, sharing it. It was good to see 17 assists."

With more positives than negatives coming out of that exhibition, the Flyers then hosted Ball State in the season opener and promptly jumped out to a 14–0 lead, holding Ball State to 0–11 shooting from the field. That lead was cut to three at halftime, and with 5.6 seconds to play, Taylor Persons of the Cardinals made a nearly uncontested layup to give Ball State a 77–76 lead.

Dayton got the ball just past mid-court, calling time-out with 1.6 seconds remaining. Bucky and I set the stage for the radio audience.

"Xeyrius will inbound. He slaps it. He looks. Looking for Darrell. He lobs and it's caught by Josh! He puts it up AND IN, AND IN, AND IN, AND IN! IT'S GOOD AND DAYTON HAS WON AT THE BUZZER!"

A disaster was averted, and the Arena erupted in celebration. Grant had won his official debut at UD as he joined me courtside after talking to the team in the locker room. I asked him about the game-winning play. "We were looking for two things," he told the listening audience, both on radio and in the Arena. "We tried to get something for Josh at the rim with 1.6 [seconds to play] or if we could free Darrell up for a catch and shoot, we felt he had time for one dribble and get a shot up. Great pass by X and an even greater catch by Josh and finish."

Perhaps lost in the euphoria of the victory were two concerns that arose. Xeyrius Williams got caught in a switch and ended up getting beat off the dribble by Taylor Persons for the go-ahead layup. Williams was unable to move adequately because of what we soon learned was a bulging disc in his back. Dayton nearly didn't have time for the game-winning play, because John Crosby momentarily froze after Persons made the shot, wasting precious seconds bringing the ball up. Was he the right guy to be running at the point?

The Flyers then traveled to South Carolina for the Gilden Charleston Classic. A loss in the first game to Hofstra still provided some optimism, as Kostas showed some potential with 10 points and 10 rebounds. Dayton bounced back with a win over Ohio U, and then had their youth and inexperience exposed with a loss to an Old Dominion team that featured a handful of fifth-year seniors.

A home win over Akron was followed by a home loss to Auburn. Xeyrius Williams was sidelined for both of those games. Dayton was literally and figuratively limping along at 3–3 heading into SEC country, at Mississippi State.

The proximity of Starkville, Mississippi, to Memphis provided an opportunity for Jalen Crutcher's family to come see him play. He had close to a dozen friends and relatives on hand, and they picked the right game to see. Crutcher made his first collegiate start and scored what was then a career-high 18 points. He did, however, have 5 turnovers, but that was part of a team-wide malaise. UD's 25 turnovers helped dig a 21-point hole in the second half, only to see the Flyers come storming back with a chance to win on their final possession. But turnover number 26 led to Quinndary Weatherspoon's layup with less than a second to play for a 61–59 Bulldogs win.

It was a heartbreaking loss, but I observed two things to come out of it that reaped tremendous dividends moving forward. Dayton had found its point guard of the present and the future. Jalen Crutcher was not perfect, but the moment was not too big for him. I can recall seasoned veterans wilting under the pressure of going back close to home and playing in front of family and friends. If he was nervous, it never showed.

Consequently, Trey Landers emerged as a leader. Our broadcast position was right by the Flyers' bench, so while I was bobbing and weaving to look around Coach Grant to see action on the court, during time-outs I had an unobstructed view of the Flyers' huddle. Trey was not happy with the focus of some of his teammates, and he let them know. His voice was heard thereafter that season, and for the rest of his UD career.

Between injuries and a lack of complete buy-in across the board, lack of depth was another issue that was revealed in the non-conference. After returning from Mississippi, the Flyers beat Tennessee Tech only to stumble badly, losing to Penn. It was the first loss to an Ivy League team in school history. Dayton then beat Georgia State in overtime. Josh Cunningham had a monster game, with 29 points in 43 minutes. Immediately following that game the team went to a hotel near the Cincinnati airport and caught an early morning flight the next day to San Francisco for a game against Saint Mary's. Josh looked like he was 100 years old, and he told me he had never been so tired in his life.

Dayton took a two-point lead into halftime, but the Gaels' experience and firepower took over in the second half, and Saint Mary's cruised to a 69–54 win. Dayton shot only 3 free throws in the game, and senior Darrell Davis was held scoreless for the first time that season. Again, Trey Landers let his displeasure with losing be heard, this time in the locker room after the game. A win back home over Wagner had the Flyers at 6–6 to end the non-conference portion of the season.

A-10 play began with a road loss at Duquesne—immaturity being part of the problem, as Kostas was goaded into a technical foul. St. Bonaventure then came to the Arena. The Bonnies were rolling along at 11–2 and were in the conversation for being an NCAA at-large team. They ended up getting in the tourney and played in the First Four at the UD Arena, beating UCLA. However, Dayton pulled off what could be considered an upset, winning 82–72 behind 28 points from Darrell Davis and 17 from Trey Landers, whose game was now speaking for itself.

Dayton then laid an egg against UMass at home. The Minutemen came in outnumbered, as first-year head coach Matt McCall, a Grant protégé, had suspended several players. A bad end to the first half and a slow start in the second half sealed the Flyers' fate. From the last three-and-a-half minutes of the first half and the first six minutes of the second (5:52 to be exact), UMass outscored UD 22–8.

Dayton bounced back with its lone road win of the year at Richmond on a Tuesday, and then had a quick turnaround for a Friday night game at home vs. VCU.

The Miami Valley got hit by snowstorm that day, so I opted to go over to the Arena in the afternoon during the shootaround practice and then just stay for the game. At the end of practice, I observed three things of note. First, Coach Grant gathered the team in a huddle and told them that the Rams would be in attack mode that night and would be looking to take the ball away every possession.

"They'll look for a weak spot," he said poking players in the chest. "Is it going to be you, or you, or you?" His tone was calm and measured, but there was a sense of urgency in his voice. Then after the players were dismissed, I noticed he took Jordan Davis aside, put his arm around him, and spoke very quietly. I asked him afterward if he was looking to build the young man's confidence up, as Davis had not been shooting the ball well. "Actually, I told him it was time for him to step up and start producing," he answered. "The days of being 'just a freshman' were over."

Third, and most revealing of things to come, Ricardo Greer was putting Obi Toppin and Jordan Pierce through extra workouts after practice was over. Obi was going hard, drill after drill. A casual observer would have thought he was busting his butt for playing time, but that was just one example of how he approached that redshirt season.

Fans would ask me, "What kind of player is that kid with the funny hair?" Obi that year had died his hair blondish red.

"All I know," I would answer, "is that he is athletic, energetic, and coachable. I think that is a pretty good recipe for success."

Greer stopped the practice and told Pierce he had to work harder. "Obi's going hard," he said. "You need to go hard, too. You can make each other better."

While Obi was working hard on his future, he later told me he was focusing on the current team's success. "I was upset that I couldn't play, but I used the year to help myself get better and help the team get better. I would go all out. My job was to prepare the guys. On game days, since I was on scout team, I knew what the other team did, so I would make the sure guys knew what the other team was doing."

Strength Coach Casey Cathrall had been working with Obi since his arrival on campus. While Flyer fans eventually saw the talent, Casey saw Toppin's work ethic. "What people don't realize is that kid would lift 90 minutes with table stretching and mobility etc., then go and be the first person in the gym shooting before practice, practice for 2 hours, and then do a 30–45-minute skill workout post-practice," he recalled. "It was pretty remarkable how much he worked and it was really his passion for basketball that drove it all. I've been around few kids in my career who love basketball as much as Obi Toppin."

That night Coach's post-practice speech paid dividends. Dayton turned the ball over just 11 times and made 17 of 32 3-pointers, including four each by Darrell Davis, Jalen Crutcher, and newly confident Jordan Davis. The final 3 by walk-on Joey Gruden sent the crowd into a frenzy as the Flyers celebrated a 106–79 rout of the Rams that wasn't even that close.

The mojo was short-lived. Dayton lost four of the next five, including a heartbreaker in double overtime at UMass. In that defeat, Coach Grant got a glimpse of better things to come.

Dayton had the ball with the score tied at the end of regulation.

"We put the ball in Jalen's hands and he drove it, made a move going to the rim, going right, spun back, and the ball rimmed in and out on him. And I remember thinking, *He wanted that. He wanted that moment to try and win the game for his team.* That game sticks out for me, but there were others in the non-conference where he showed he was the type of guy who wanted to step up and make plays for his team."

The Flyers then avenged their earlier loss to Duquesne with an 88–73 win at home, shooting a sizzling 83% from the field in the second half. Next up was VCU and a chance to sweep the Rams. Trailing by 15 with three and a half minutes to play, the Flyers went on a 16–1 run to force overtime, but lost 88–84. Justin Tillman was unstoppable for VCU with 37 points. Grant used only 7 players in the game. Jalen Crutcher played 44 minutes, Jordan

Davis 42, Trey Landers 41, Darrell Davis 40, and Josh Cunningham 37. Matej Svoboda played 16 off the bench and John Crosby 5. Kostas and Xeyrius Williams were noticeable by their absence. It was obvious that Grant was going with a "coalition of the willing."

After that VCU loss, the Flyers went 3–3 the rest of the way to finish the season at 14–16, 8–10 in the Atlantic 10. Xeyrius Williams played in only one game in that stretch, shutting down due to lingering back issues.

Dayton went to Washington DC for the A-10 Championship, needing four wins in four days as the only chance of post-season play. Again, they faced their rival, VCU, and came up short, losing 77–72. A string of 12 consecutive winning seasons came to an end. It was a bitter pill to swallow for the Flyer Faithful, coming off four straight trips to the NCAA Tournament.

There is no doubt in my mind that Dayton could have won more games that year—not necessarily a 20- win season with post-season potential, but a winning season. It would have been a hollow achievement. Anthony Grant could have turned a blind eye to inconsistent efforts, bad habits, and a lack of buy-in from some individuals and eked out a few more victories. Rules needed to be established and enforced to create a culture of sustainable success by any measurement.

There was, however, reason for optimism. Jalen Crutcher was named to the Atlantic Ten All-Rookie Team. Trey Landers finished the year with six consecutive games scoring in double figures, after scoring just 27 points his entire freshman year. Darrell Davis graduated, after scoring 1,008 points in his career, and Josh Cunningham would be back for one more year of reliable work.

Now it was time to build a full roster.

**Flyers outside restaurant in
Springfield, MA in December 2018**

06

MOVING IN THE RIGHT DIRECTION

A LITTLE OVER TWO MONTHS AFTER closing the 2017–2018 season with a loss to VCU in the A-10 tournament, Anthony Grant joined me for an extended live interview on *Miami Valley's Morning News*, the show I host on WHIO Radio in addition to my duties calling UD football and basketball games. It had been a busy eight weeks for Grant and his staff, in some ways more of a whirlwind and certainly more critical than that same period the year previous when he first got the job.

The roster was going through a metamorphosis. On March 11, 2018, just three days after the VCU game, Xeyrius Williams announced he was transferring. It was no shock, as he had shut down for the final two weeks and had already cleaned out his locker. Soon thereafter, Jordan Pierce and John Crosby entered the transfer portal, Kostas entered the NBA draft, and Matej Svoboda opted to return to the

Czech Republic and play pro basketball there.

It proved to be a good move for all five. Kostas was the final player taken in the NBA draft that spring by Dallas and played two games with the Mavericks, spending the rest of the 2018–2019 season in the G-League. He then signed with the Lakers and spent this past season with their G-League team. Matej averaged 17.6 points a game for Svitavy in the Czech Republic–Mattoni NBL. Jordan Pierce was not an A-10 caliber player, and after a year at Odessa Junior College he had an injury-plagued season at Tennessee-Martin, appearing in 18 games. Xeyrius Williams and John Crosby both had to sit a year before making the most of their final season of college basketball. Williams went to Akron, where the Zips won the MAC East and he was Third-Team All MAC, averaging 13.9 points and 9.5 rebounds a game. John Crosby averaged 35 minutes a game at Delaware State and averaged 19.7 points a game, good enough for Second-Team All MEAC honors.

It irks me that some Dayton fans chose to vilify these guys once they no longer wore a Flyer uniform. I can appreciate frustration and/or disappointment in their productivity in the 2017–18 season, but I could only wish them well, and I am truly happy for them in the success they found elsewhere. At the time they chose to leave, the University of Dayton was not a good fit for them: not for them, and not for UD.

I began that interview back on May 11, 2018, asking Coach Grant about "fit." Anthony replied,

> I told our guys at the beginning of
> the season, really in the summer, our
> culture was the most important thing
> of anything else we did. We had to
> establish our identity. Who we are,

who we aspire to be, and the way we
are going to be about doing that. At
different stages of the year you figure
out who fits that culture we are trying
to establish, not good or bad, it's not
always a good fit.

With those departures, Dayton had Josh Cunningham returning for his senior year, Trey Landers was
a rising junior coming off his first productive season
on the court, and Ryan Mikesell was also classified as
a junior, having spent the previous season rehabbing
from double hip surgery. Jalen Crutcher and Jordan
Davis were sophomores, having appeared in every
game as freshmen. Academic redshirt Obi Toppin
was ready to make his debut as a freshman. So, the
Flyers had just four players who had played meaningful minutes the previous season, plus Ryan and Obi,
who had been part of the team all year.

When the season ended, Grant and his staff knew
of two players who would be added to the ranks.
Dwayne Cohill would come in as a freshman after
scoring 2,182 points in his high school career at Holy
Name, just outside of Cleveland. "At the end of my
junior year, Coach [Grant] came down to see me play
in Texas," Cohill told me. "Coach Solomon was very
important in the process and was one of the main reasons I came to UD."

Ricardo Greer again tapped into his background to
land a second recruit. He grew up in the Washington
Heights neighborhood of New York City. His parents
were both natives of the Dominican Republic.

Greer signed 6'6" guard Jhery Matos from Mon-
roe College, a junior college in Brooklyn. Matos had
made a verbal commitment to come to UD, where he
would have two seasons of eligibility. Matos is a native

of the Dominican Republic and spent his final two years of high school in Florida, before attending junior college the past two years. "He's a guy I think our fans will fall in love with, because he plays with such energy. Very unselfish guy. I think he understands what it takes to win," Grant told me on the air.

With eight scholarship players on the roster, Dayton had five spots available. In April, Frankie Policelli from Long Island signed, thanks to an assist from my broadcast partner, Bucky. When Ricardo Greer was talking to Frankie's dad, he recalled his days growing up in Syracuse watching NBA games between the Nationals and the visiting Cincinnati Royals. The elder Policelli was impressed with the hard-nosed play of Oscar Robertson's running mate Arlen "Bucky" Bockhorn. Greer told him Bucky was still involved in the radio broadcast, and when the family came for a visit to Dayton, Bucky joined them for lunch.

The addition of Cohill, Matos, and Policelli improved the numbers in the short term, but again Grant and the staff were thinking big picture. "We made a decision as a staff that going into year two we could either sign guys who could be immediately eligible and could add to our team, or take a chance and bring in a group that we knew would not be able to play in year two. But with what we had in the program, we believed their talent and their character could elevate things significantly," he told me that spring.

The first of those pieces was Ibi Watson. Originally recruited by Archie Miller when he was at UD, Watson opted to go to Michigan out of Pickerington Central High School, just east of Columbus. He appeared in 19 games as freshman and was part of the Wolverines team that advanced to the National Title game as a sophomore. But he had averaged only 5.2 minutes a game when he decided to transfer. Within an hour of his name appearing in the transfer portal, Dayton reached out. "My tenth-grade year, Archie offered me a scholarship after I came to a team camp," Ibi told me. "When I decided to transfer, Coach Slo reached out to me and I visited campus. I knew this was a high major program with great fan support, so I would not be dropping down a level to come here."

Grant liked what he was getting in Watson. "He's a great young man, first and foremost. He's got a tremendous work ethic in terms of his desire to be the kind of guy to impact the program," Grant said. "He's got a great skill set in terms of his ability to shoot the basketball. Obviously, playing at Michigan and going through practice every day and the experience he got there add a level of maturity and hunger, really, to get out on the court."

While Watson was seeking a transfer in search of playing time, Rodney Chatman had a different motivation to leave Chattanooga and come to Dayton. He had appeared in all 30 games as a freshman, starting 2, and started 29 out of 30 as a sophomore. Chatman first considered transferring after his freshman year when Matt McCall, who recruited him, went to UMass. He decided to stay, and despite the ample playing time, "I just didn't like the way things were heading, so I thought it was best to leave," he later shared with me.

His dad, Rodney, reached out to Coach Grant. They had first met when Chatman was coaching at New Smyrna Beach and Grant recruited his star player LaDarius Halton to come to Florida. Grant said the younger Chatman's track record at Chattanooga showed he had the ability to play at a high level. "You look at this numbers in terms of his scoring, his assist-to-turnover ratio, his ability to rebound," Grant continued. "On the defensive end, he's a guy who can put some pressure on your opponent and impact the game on that side of the ball as well."

When he came for his visit, all parties agreed it was a good fit. "The University, our administration, did a great job on the visit of making sure he understood the commit we have to our student athletes on and off the floor," Grant said. "He and his family felt comfortable and he made the decision to join us."

If Rodney and his family felt comfortable on the visit, the point guard knew he had made the right decision that summer when he moved in on campus. "Ibi and Jalen [Crutcher] started helping me move my stuff in and we just hung out the rest of the day. We became friends, just like that."

The final addition came after that radio interview in May. Jordy Tshimanga, 6'11" and 268 pounds, was born in Montreal to parents from the Congo. He finished his high school career in Boston, and his coach knew Ricardo Greer. Jordy played two seasons at Nebraska, and when the assistant coach with whom he had a close relationship left Lincoln, he too decided to leave. He made his visit to Dayton in August and then committed immediately. "I just wanted to get the process over with and I saw I could be a good fit," Jordy said. "It clicked right away. I'm an extrovert. I like seeing people smile. Since I first set foot on campus, students and teachers have made me feel welcome."

Jordy literally announced his presence with authority. At a cookout for the men's and women's teams as well as booster and athletic department members hosted by Dr. Steve Levitt, each player was asked to take the microphone and introduce themselves to the crowd (I think 2,500 people qualifies as a crowd!). Jordy greeted them in French, one of four languages he speaks, and then said he was a point guard. He then proceeded to spend the afternoon fetching plates of food for ladies seated under the big tents.

While Watson, Chatman, and Tshimanga were pieces in a big-picture puzzle, the focus was also on the task at hand—getting Ryan Mikesell and Obi Toppin integrated into the lineup after a year on the sidelines.

"The thing that gets lost is how difficult that was for Ryan," Grant said. "To not only go through double hip surgery, but to be without the game, have it taken away from him. And I think his appreciation for not only playing, but competing and impacting his teammates . . . he may have developed a stronger appreciation for how quickly things can change for you."

While Ryan was sitting out, he did very little "sitting."

"I've never had a guy work this hard," said Dayton Basketball Strength and Conditioning Coach Casey Cathrall, as he looked back on that year. "Ryan literally started with exercises I would give for my grandmother to start off with after coming off of his bilateral hip labrum repairs. It's really incredible where he started and how much sustained success he has had considering his hips. It's truly a testament to the type of kid Ryan is and his work ethic he brings. Most consistent worker I've ever had in my career."

He also had to adjust mentally to sitting out. "The first game of the season, I pretty much embraced being a player-coach," recalled Mikesell. "During games I am always talking to the guys about [the other team's] personnel and defensive assignments."

He was part of every film session and scouting report, but he was able to learn even more while forced to be an observer during the games. "I really understand now the importance of each possession, he told me. "You don't realize that when you are playing."

Ryan made quite a splash as a freshman, scoring a career-best 21 points vs. Southeast Missouri State in his very first collegiate game. He appeared in 22 games, averaging 3.0 per game. As a sophomore, he appeared in all 32 games, starting 24, but he was physically limited by his hip issues, which gave him pain and limited his mobility. He was honest with his coaches and told them he was having a hard time defending. Plus, it was affecting his shot. "I was in pain, so I had a hard time loading up. It's all connected."

If Grant felt good about Mikesell's ability to play again, when it came to Toppin, it was more about turning him loose after a year of watching. In the May 11, 2018, interview with Coach Grant on WHIO Radio, I said: "When people ask me about Obi Toppin, I tell them he is athletic, energetic, and coachable. Is that accurate?" Grant replied,

> I think you hit the nail on the head. Obi is a guy who took advantage of the year to matriculate academically and athletically. Obi came in, I think 6'8" about 190 pounds. He's grown an inch and put on about 25 to 30 pounds of weight.
>
> I think the thing that Obi brings, is he is the same guy every day. He's a high-motor, high-energy guy who loves to compete. He's a guy who his teammates really enjoy being around. A guy that plays with great enthusiasm, who loves the game, and I think it really shows in everything he does, whether competitively on the court, or just being a guy walking around campus.

There was also a staff change heading into the 2018–2019 season. James Kane had left to rejoin former Murray State Coach Steve Prohm at Iowa State. Donnie Jones was hired, having spent the previous year on staff at Wichita State. He had been a scout for the NBA's Los Angeles Clippers in 2016–2017 after being let go by Central Florida. He was the head coach at UCF for six years and for three years at Marshall. He first met Grant at Marshall in 1994 when Billy Donavan became the Head Coach of the Thundering Herd. Jones stayed on from the previous staff and was sent to the airport to pick up Grant for his interview with Donavan.

"He thought I was a manager," Jones remembered. "And I will never let him forget that!"

In 1996 Donavan became the Head Coach at Florida and took Jones and Grant with him. They were joined by Darren Hertz as a student coach and were all there for the National Championship years of 2006 and 2007.

When Jones arrived at UD, it was a homecoming. "I walked through the door and I already had chemistry with Darren and Ricardo. I had hired Ricardo when I was the head coach at UCF and had told him to reach out to Anthony when he got the job in Dayton," Jones said. "I knew Slo [Anthony Solomon] and you add in Andy [Farrell] and we all bonded. Team chemistry starts with the staff."

The chemistry among the staff soon included the team. Jones said it was willful and intentional on the part of Coach Grant and the other coaches. "Believe-in comes before buy-in. We talked to the guys and shared our stories with them, as we wanted to learn their stories, not necessarily basketball related. Coach preached 'let our work be the process that gives us an unfair advantage over the competition.'"

The change in the team was dramatic when Dayton played an exhibition game against Capital, coached by Anthony's former Flyer teammate Damon Goodwin. I brought it up right away in the post-game radio interview. "My big takeaway from this tonight, I think it is obvious and almost palpable—this team likes each other."

Grant responded, "From the time they got together this summer, it was pretty evident that they got along really well, and we talked about it all off-season. They bonded really well, they play together, they play for each other. Four of our nine that played tonight, it was their first time playing in front of our fans, playing Division I college basketball. Every experience like this is very valuable."

The seeds of a winning culture were sprouting in the chemistry and unselfish manner this group of Flyers played with in that 89–71 exhibition win over Capital. The coming-out party for an eventual superstar came in the season opener vs. North Florida.

Senior Josh Cunningham injured an ankle in practice and was unable to play. Obi Toppin got the start in his first official collegiate game and responded with a double-double of 18 points and 10 rebounds in a 78–70 win over the Ospreys, including 4 first-half dunks.

Dayton followed up with wins over Coppin State and Fort Wayne before heading to the Bahamas for the Bad Boys Mowers Battle for Atlantis. All the teams stayed at, the tournament venue, the massive Atlantis resort. Josh Postorino worked the games with me on radio and we spent the first few days hanging out with fans and boosters while attending press conferences and watching the Flyers practice. The team had a good vibe about them, and the guys had a good time going down the water slides and hanging out by the pool and beach during their free time.

The first game was against Butler, and Dayton jumped on the Bulldogs early, leading by 11 at halftime and as much as 15 in the second half. Butler made a run late, but Jalen Crutcher and Dwayne Cohill each made a pair of free throws in the final 25 seconds to ice a 69–64 win. Winning the first game in these 3-game exempt tournaments is crucial, as you know you will not get skunked and will come away with at least one win.

Unfortunately, that was the case. The Flyers lost to eventual National Champion Virginia 66–59, but trailed by just 4 with under 2 minutes to play. The next game provided another missed opportunity at a signature win. After trailing by 6 at the half, Dayton led Oklahoma 41–34 before hitting a scoring drought and falling 65–54. In addition to losing the game, Jhery Matos injured his toe. He was in a boot and then had an eventual season-ending surgery. Dayton had planned on redshirting Frankie Policelli, but with Matos out, UD was down to eight scholarship players, so Frankie made his season debut back home against 25th-ranked Mississippi State.

Dayton led 51–44 with 6:19 to play, but Mississippi State ended the game with a 21–7 run to win by seven, 65–58. Three games in a row against quality opponents: three games in a row the Flyers had a chance to win. Three games in a row they came up empty.

Coach Grant looked back on that stretch. "Coming out of that tournament [in the Bahamas] I felt pretty good about our team. When we were right, I thought we could compete with anyone on our schedule. The Mississippi State loss was disappointing because we had a lead late and let it get away."

The Flyers crushed Detroit Mercy 98–59; Obi set

a school record with 8 dunks in the game. After trailing by 19 at the half, Dayton ended up losing 82–72 at 8th-ranked Auburn, another eventual Final Four team, and then took a trip to Connecticut to face Tulsa in the Basketball Hall of Fame Showcase at the Mohegan Sun Casino.

The day before the game, Keith Waleskowski, who was working the game on radio with me, and I joined the team for dinner at a restaurant in Springfield, Massachusetts, followed by a private tour of the Basketball Hall of Fame. The players got to shoot at a Naismith-style peach basket, and 5'7" walk-on Camron Greer posed next to a cutout of Muggsy Bogues to show he was actually taller.

The next day was the most disappointing game of the season, from my perspective. There were more heartbreaking losses and there were even more lopsided losses, but for the first and fortunately last time all-season, I thought Dayton not only didn't play as a team but also didn't show a great effort. A 72–67 loss to Tulsa left a bitter taste in everyone's mouth, made worse when plane problems kept us from getting back to Dayton that night.

"I felt we had some opportunities that year that we didn't take advantage of. And sometimes as a team you have to go through some stuff, get some scars, get wounded before you can appreciate how fragile winning and losing can be," recalled Grant.

Dayton beat Western Michigan and Presbyterian heading into Christmas. The Flyers somewhat limped into the break, beating the Blue Hose by 12 after racing out to a 45–17 halftime lead. In the first game back after the holiday, a pretty good Georgia Southern team came to the Arena. Dayton led by 13 at the break and by as much as 16 early in the second half, but it took a pair of Trey Landers's rebounds—one

at the offensive end and one at the defensive end—
to seal the victory. On the post-game radio interview,
Coach Grant was not happy:

> That's back-to-back games where we
> have been unimpressive—uninspired
> in the second half. As a basketball
> team we have to hold ourselves a lot
> more accountable in terms of our
> competitive character, in terms of
> not being complacent, in terms of
> not being offended when another
> team makes a run at us. That's an
> area we need to work on to get better
> at that.

The long-term story from that game is not the
blown lead or the clutch plays that saved victory.
About midway through Georgia Southern's comeback, Dayton had a 6-point lead when Jalen Crutcher
corralled a rebound. Here's what happened next on
radio:

"He throws it ahead to Obeeee—Oh, my God!—
between the legs . . . and a helicopter jam!" It was
more like a windmill dunk, and the crowd went absolutely ballistic, even more than I had on the air.

Georgia Southern called a time-out and as Dayton
headed to the bench, Coach Grant met Obi halfway
there. They had an earnest one-sided conversation
during the entire time-out.

"I talked to him about being aware of the score
and time, and how a play like that can motivate an
opponent," Grant explained on his weekly radio show
a few days after the game. "Myself and everyone in
the program had probably seen him complete that
dunk at least ten times in practice. He probably had

some behind doors that were even more spectacular than that. Time and score and respect for opponent."

The message was taken to heart. A few games into the A-10 season Dayton won in double overtime at UMass. At a critical point in the back-and-forth game, Obi made a cut to the basket and was wide open on a lob, but instead of dunking it, he laid the ball in the basket as if he was putting a baby down to sleep in a crib. He was very aware of the time and score.

Dayton entered conference play with an 8–5 record and won the A-10 opener at home over Richmond. Next up was George Washington on the road. Kostas was in DC, as his Texas Legends G-League team had a game against the Capital City Go-Go's. The Flyers went as a group to watch him the night before.

The next day at shootaround, Ryan Mikesell and Obi Toppin both went over and sat with trainer Mike Mulcahey almost as soon at the practice began. They were complaining of being light-headed and nauseous and sat out the rest of the workout.

With the prospect of playing with only six healthy scholarship players, Coach Grant addressed the team:

"Just focus on what you need to do. Maybe some of you will have to play more minutes, but don't be trying to do more than what you are capable of doing."

Fortunately, both players felt better that afternoon. Unfortunately, the Flyers fell behind by 22 in the first half as the Colonials hit their first 10 shots. With the starting unit not getting things done, Coach Grant threw Obi Toppin, Dwayne Cohill, and Frankie Policelli into the game. They were part of an 8–0 run, with Cohill and Policelli each hitting a three, and by halftime UD had closed the gap, GW leading 40–30. When the Colonials started the second half on a 7–0 run, things again looked bleak.

And then Jordan Davis caught fire. He scored Dayton's first 8 points of the half and hit a 3 to give the Flyers their first lead, with just under 10 minutes to play. Davis hit 7 threes and had a career-high 25 points, as Jalen Crutcher and Trey Landers put the game away with a combined 6-for-6 free throws in the final minute for a 72–66 win. Dayton matched its road win total of the previous season.

After the game I talked to Coach Grant on WHIO Radio. "It might have been the worst start I have seen in a college basketball game, but might have been one of the better comebacks as well."

Grant chuckled, "You definitely never want to start that way. I thought in the first half, give our young guys credit—Dwyane, Frankie, Obi—those guys came in and gave us energy."

He then went on to praise the work of Jordan Davis. "It was great to see him get some shots to fall. He shot the ball with a high amount of confidence. And like any shooter, once you see the ball go in, you feel good and you get into a rhythm. I thought our guys did a good job of finding him in the second half. Guys just played with unbelievable heart and determination. Great job defensively. It's a huge win."

The Flyers followed that up with a home win over UMass and then came the first of two showdowns with VCU in Richmond. The Flyers were riding a six-game winning streak that began just before Christmas. VCU had developed into a rivalry, with the fire stoked by their fans on social media. One of the things that Shaka Smart had done before he left there for Texas was lobby the A-10 to have Dayton and VCU in the same pod each season, because he felt the fans of both teams deserved to have a home game in the series each year.

Dayton was playing well. Jalen Crutcher, Josh Cunningham, and Trey Landers were consistent. Obi Toppin was getting better every game, and Ryan Mikesell was doing all of the little things well. Jordan Davis had followed up his career-high 25 at George Washington with 21 in the UMass win and was the reigning A-10 Player of the Week heading into the game against the Rams.

The matchup was as good as anticipated. VCU had a 1-point lead at the half. In the second half Davis hit a 3 to give the Flyers a lead, and then back and forth it went, with the game tied 9 times in the second half including 69–69 with 33 seconds to play. Marcus Evans hit a 3 for the Rams and iced the game at the line with 4 free throws for a 76–71 VCU win. Jordan Davis finished with 17 points, the third game in a row that he led the Flyers in scoring.

Davis played the role of hero again in the following game, an 89–86 win at St. Bonaventure in double overtime. When Jalen Crutcher fouled out in the first overtime, Davis had to play point guard in the second OT. He made a costly turnover, but then hit a floater and then a 3 with 15 seconds to play to secure the road win. Ryan Mikesell led six Flyers in double figures, matching his career high with 21. At 12–6, 4–1 in the A-10, UD was starting to build some momentum.

The momentum proved to be fleeting as the Flyers returned home to face George Mason. In another back-and-forth game with 13 lead changes, Dayton went scoreless the final 3 minutes of the game and lost 67–63. GMU had a 2-point lead with 10 seconds to play when Jalen Crutcher's 3-point attempt rattled out. Again, he showed he was the type of player who wanted to take that shot.

The Flyers then ran off 3 straight wins, at Fordham and then against Saint Joseph's and Duquesne at home. Dayton trailed the Dukes by 8 at the half before Obi Toppin put on a show, scoring a then career-high 26 points. Next up was a trip to Saint Louis. Dayton fell behind 10–0 early and trailed by 17 in the second half before falling 73–60, the biggest margin of defeat all season. Saint Louis killed UD on the glass, pulling down 19 offensive rebounds.

That Tuesday game was followed by a Saturday road game at Rhode Island. The defending A-10 Champion Rams had a new look after graduating a talented senior class but were not without weapons. Jeff Dowtin and Fatts Russell were thought to be one of the better backcourts in the A-10, and Cyril Langevine was a powerful rebounder, a weakness Dayton had revealed in the previous game. Even though the Flyers had a better record than URI, I thought it would be an uphill battle. I could not have been more wrong. Dayton dominated every facet of the game and led from wire to wire for a 77–48 win. Jalen Crutcher abused Fatts Russell, scoring a team-high 20 points while holding Russell scoreless.

Now 16–8 overall and 8–3 in the league, Dayton had a big opportunity with a home rematch against VCU. Dayton found itself down by 12 at the half, and when the Rams went on a 10–0 to start the second half to take the lead out to 22, the Flyers began their most impressive comeback of the year, even more than the game at George Washington, given the quality of the opponent they were facing. Jalen Crutcher sparked an 8–0 run with a pair of 3-pointers. VCU responded and the same type of see-saw game that we saw in Richmond ensued. Obi Toppin scored in the final minute to give Dayton a 68–67 lead, but Marcus Evans broke the Flyers' heart for the second time that season with a go-ahead layup with just 6 seconds to play. Afterward Coach Grant was as pleased in a loss as I had ever heard him on his post-game radio show.

"I couldn't be prouder of the fight our guys showed," he said. "They showed a lot of character coming back from 22 like that. Our guys fought and battled all the way through."

Still with 9 in the loss column and no signature wins, Dayton's at-large NCAA chances were on life support heading to Davidson. The focus was now on trying to secure one of the top four spots in the A-10 Championship in Brooklyn. The Flyers took a big step toward that with a 74–73 win over the Davidson Wildcats on Josh Cunningham's free throw with 2.2 seconds to play. Before the game I noticed that the writer that was seated next to Brooks Hall and me on press row was from an Austrian basketball magazine. Davidson's freshman center, Luka Brajkovic, was from the western part of that country. The writer was shocked when I addressed him in German. I had spent my sophomore year in college at the University of Salzburg, and had actually played on a local club basketball team while in school there. Brooks had played pro basketball in Austria along with another former Flyer Sean Finn, and he and the writer had some common acquaintances.

Buoyed by the win at Davidson, the Flyers avenged their earlier Saint Louis loss with a 70–62 home victory and then completed a two-game sweep of UMass with a 72–48 rout in Amherst. However, they could not pull off the sweep of Rhode Island, losing 72–70 at the Arena in overtime. Jalen Crutcher missed a clean look from 3 at the end of regulation. Here's what it sounded like on WHIO Radio:

"Crutcher from 3. Good if it goes, it does not. Tapped in by Landers and OH! IT JUST ROLLED OFF! A tap by Trey Landers just rolled off as the buzzer sounded!"

On his post-game interview, Coach Grant said the Flyers lost the game well before that tap-in failed to fall.

"The game shouldn't have come down to the last few possessions. Characteristic of the way we played, 19 turnovers today. We didn't bring our best and we needed to bring our best, especially down the stretch here with everything that was at stake."

Dayton finished with a home win over LaSalle and a road win at Duquesne to end the regular season at 21–10, 13–5 in the A-10—good enough for the third seed and a first-round bye in the league tournament. Before the team left for Brooklyn, the A-10 announced its post-season awards. Obi Toppin was named Rookie of the Year and First Team All-Conference, the first freshman to do that since Lamar Odom at Rhode Island in 1999. Jalen Crutcher and Josh Cunningham both received Third Team All-Conference Honors, and Ryan Mikesell was named to the All-Academic Team.

Upon arriving in New York, Dayton knew their only chance at an NCAA Tournament berth was to win the A-10 tourney. They would have to wait to see who their opponent would be in the quarterfinals. Saint Louis and Richmond met on Thursday for the chance to play Dayton on Friday. The Flyers had split in the regular season with the Billikens and had defeated Richmond in their only matchup.

Saint Louis pulled out a 71–68 win over the Spiders and took that little piece of momentum into the Friday afternoon game vs. UD. Obi Toppin, playing in his hometown as the reigning A-10 Rookie of the Year, made a 3-pointer early in the game and held up three fingers triumphantly to the supportive crowd. But he soon tweaked his knee and never looked to be right after that. He finished with just 7 points, and the Flyers—after leading by one at the half—watched the Billikens pull away for a 64–55 win. To Saint Louis's credit, they went on to beat Davidson and then St. Bonaventure to win the automatic berth in the NCAA Tournament—four wins in four days!

The call from the NIT came Sunday night and Dayton, seeded fifth, would play at fourth-seeded Colorado on Tuesday night. It was a quick turnaround and a late starting game at 9:00 p.m. Mountain Time, which had it tipping off past 11:00 p.m. in Dayton. Travel arrangements were put together quickly, and with no room on the charter flight, my color analyst for the game, Josh Postorino, three managers, and I had to fly commercial to Denver and then rent a van for the trip to Boulder. Trey Landers also took the late-day flight with us on Monday, as he had to attend the funeral of a relative killed in a car crash.

We arrived on the Colorado campus in time for Trey to join the team practice, and then finally about 8:00 local time, but 10:00 my stomach's time, checked into the hotel and had some dinner. One thing I noticed at practice that night and the next day at shootaround were the constant reminders to visiting teams of the elevation and its effect on oxygen levels.

When game time arrived, McKinley Wright, who had signed with Dayton but opted to go to Colorado after the coaching change, was coming off a stellar sophomore year in the Pac-12. He visited with Landers, Josh Cunningham, and Ryan Mikesell before the game, as they no doubt had become friends during his UD recruitment.

Some might point to the elevation or the quick turnaround or even the experimental rules the NIT used in the game—3-point line farther back, lane widened, shot clock reset to 20 after an offensive rebound, team fouls reset at 10-minute mark—as causing Dayton to lose the game 78–73. In reality, McKinley Wright beat the Flyers. He scored 19 points and had 5 assists, but the stats don't show how he took control of the game and eventually put his team on his back for the win. I am sure that some Flyer fans were wondering "what if" Wright was at the helm for Dayton instead of the man who replaced him, Jalen Crutcher. Anyone who had access to a crystal ball at the time would have not made that trade.

The Flyers closed out the season in round one of the NIT, but the development of the tandem of Jalen Crutcher and Obi Toppin, along with the leadership of Trey Landers and Ryan Mikesell, had Dayton well positioned to take the next step—if not a leap—forward. Now it was time to add some more pieces.

**Trainer Mike Mulcahey & Larry at
post-tornado food distribution**

07

A DIFFICULT SUMMER

EARLY IN THE MORNING AFTER THE NIT loss to Colorado, the team managers, Josh Postorino, and I drove from Boulder to the airport in Denver for the flight back home. Leaving for the airport at 4:00 a.m. is never fun (unless you are going on vacation!). Traveling after a loss is never fun. Traveling after a season-ending loss at four in the morning is the worst.

Nevertheless, I was somewhat glad to close the chapter on the 2018–2019 season, because I saw the promise of what could be the following year. I was not alone in my optimism. Fans were buzzing about the guys then sitting out who would then be eligible to play in 2019–2020. Chase Johnson had joined the team, transferring from Florida shortly after Christmas following a concussion-plagued year and a half at Florida. He enrolled for the second semester and was cleared to begin practicing. By the end of the season, Jhery Matos was cleared to practice after his December toe surgery. That created a scout team of

Johnson, Matos, Jordy Tshimanga, Ibi Watson, and Rodney Chatman. Apocryphal stories of that team regularly beating the starters in practice were widely circulated among fans. I never witnessed such events, but I watched enough to realize that each of them would be an impactful player. Watson had a smooth shot and could score in a variety of ways. Chatman had extremely long arms that would enable him to be a lock-down defender and showed quickness up and down the floor that reminded me at times of London Warren, a.k.a. "The Jacksonville Jet." Tshimanga showed good footwork around the basket, and a soft shooting touch. Johnson was athletic and showed some shooting range. Fans already got a taste of the type of defender and Swiss Army knife–type of player Matos could be from his brief early season appearance.

One incoming freshman would be added to that mix. Moulaye Sissoko was a 6'9" powerful post player who was from Mali, in north central Africa, and had played high school basketball first at Central Park Christian in Birmingham, Alabama, and then at Lincoln Academy in Atlanta, Georgia. Then–Strength Coach Ed Streit always took a picture of freshmen as he began working with them and a picture at the end of the summer to provide a "before-and-after" comparison. Streit said that Moo (as he became known among his teammates) was the first freshman he ever worked with who had no need of the "before" picture.

Beyond graduating Josh Cunningham, there were two other departures. Frankie Policelli asked for his release to enter the transfer portal. That was understandable, as he averaged only 4.8 minutes per game, appearing in 20 of the Flyers' 33 games. In a late February game at UMass, he played just 5 minutes in a blowout win. His mom was all smiles after the game, talking to the other players and their families. His dad, however, just glared at the coaching staff.

Jordan Davis also decided to transfer.

"I met with the whole team as a group after we got back from Colorado," said Coach Grant later. "We talked about what was expected of them moving forward and I said if anyone wanted to talk to me individually they were welcome to do that. Jordan came in my office and said that after talking things over with his family, he decided it would be in his best interest to leave."

Davis had started 32 of 33 games, with walk-on Jack Westerfield getting the start instead on Senior Day. Perhaps he saw his playing time becoming diminished. He is an extremely quiet guy: polite, but not very talkative, and he rarely displayed any emotion on-or-off the court. However, his body language was not that of a happy person.

Shortly after Frankie and Jordan announced they were transferring—Policelli eventually to Stony Brook and Davis to Middle Tennessee State—I saw them with their soon-to-be former teammates at a festival of sorts on campus in which they were running carnival-like games for fellow students. There could not have been much acrimony in their departure.

There was one more change that spring. On March 29, 2019, Donnie Jones was named the new Head Coach at Stetson University in Deland, Florida, leaving after just one year on the Dayton staff. It was, however, a year in which he was impactful on the Flyer program and the program earned a place in his heart.

Jones thought Dayton was on the precipice of something good.

"We were really close. I thought we were one player away. We just needed that depth. Not everyone was totally bought in, but we didn't have another guy. Through it all Coach Grant was consistent in winning and losing."

Donnie also felt the chemistry among the staff and vibe between the staff and the players did not need to be disrupted. He recommended to Coach Grant that he not go outside looking for a replacement. Anthony did not, opting to promote Darren Hertz from within.

James Haring joined the staff as the Director of Basketball Operations. After working for four years as a team manager under Bob Huggins at West Virginia, he was a graduate assistant at Illinois and served another season under John Groce as director of basketball operations. He held that same position at Jacksonville State in Alabama for two seasons before joining the Flyers.

I asked Haring what attracted him to come to Dayton. "Being from just south of Chicago [New Lenox, Illinois], Dayton has a brand, and I was familiar with Dayton since I was a kid. Everyone in college basketball talks about how big-time the environment is at Dayton, the support, and how good the program has been, really throughout its time. Not just recently but in the '80s, '70s, '60s and before that. And then on top of that everyone I heard about Coach Grant as a person, him as a coach, him as a leader; it's what drew me here."

After two years as a grad assistant, Brett Comer was named Director of Player Development. Comer had played point guard on the "Dunk City" Florida Gulf Coast team that went to the Sweet Sixteen in 2015. "I wanted to get into coaching, and an assistant at Florida Gulf Coast called James Kane, who knew my fiancée's brother. I was also familiar with Coach Grant and Coach Hertz," he told me. "I didn't know a ton about the history of Dayton. I was familiar with Scooch and the teams that had recent success, because that was the same time I was playing."

Sean Damaska, a former tight end on the Indiana football team, was heading into his second year as a graduate assistant. Khyle Marshall, who had played on Butler's Final Four team, joined Damaska as a graduate assistant, and both were valuable as scout team players, putting some muscle on Dayton's big men in practice.

The roster was set, and it appeared depth would be no issue. The staff was largely intact and were already familiar with the players. The players were already familiar with each other, even though five of them had spent the previous season in street clothes on game days and Moo was still in high school. The summer now provided the opportunity to develop chemistry and takes some classes to stay on pace to graduate.

On May 28, 2019, I drove to work on that Tuesday morning anticipating a typical day following a three-day Memorial Day weekend. Since 2003 I have been the host of *Miami Valley's Morning News* on WHIO Radio. It is my main focus, with Flyer football and basketball play-by-play a passion, but not my full-time job. I wake up each morning at 2:20 a.m.—and yes, that feels early still to me after all these years. I am usually on the road by 3:00 and arrive at our studios on South Main Street in Dayton around 3:25 a.m. Upon arrival I sort through emails, the AP wire, and news websites before meeting with my fellow team members at 4:00 a.m. As the host, I am the link between our news anchors, Brittany Otto and Chris Collins, our traffic reporter, Sgt. Mark Bowron, as well as the contributions of the Channel 7 meteorologists, and the guy who helps us prepare each morning and fills in anchoring, Bill Scheidel. John Tisdell, the halftime host of Flyer football and basketball, brings all of the elements to air through his spot in Master Control.

Nothing seemed awry on that Tuesday morning until I arrived in the parking lot and noticed an unusual number of cars. When I entered the news room it was a hubbub of activity, and once I turned on my computer I did not have to scroll very far through a long string of emails to realize what had happened.

The previous evening and into the early morning hours, fifteen tornadoes had wreaked a path of destruction across the Miami Valley. The largest that ripped through Trotwood, Brookville, Riverside, and Old North Dayton was rated an EF-4 with winds up to 170 miles per hour. I live well to the south of that, and although my wife and daughter saw the warnings on TV and sought shelter in our basement, they did not wake me up. I slept through the whole thing.

When I gathered with my colleagues that morning, we quickly became aware just how bad it was. Chris and Brittany had seen some of the damage. Brittany drove past snow plows that were pushing large trees and other debris off I-75. Chris could tell there was some damage, but the extent was still covered by darkness. As we sprang into action, Chris quickly volunteered to go back out and report from the field what was going on. Like me, he is a fulltime newsman but is also the fine play-by-play voice of Wright State Raiders basketball. He channeled those skills to describe what daylight revealed to our listeners:

> When I first when out, I went to Wagner Ford Road and 75. DP & L crews were working on the power lines. I saw the Marathon station completely destroyed. There was twisted metal, and the gas pumps had been pulled

up. Later in the morning, I saw a church steeple that had been blown down. I saw a gigantic two-by-four that had been thrown from across Miller Lane and embedded into a house.

To this day, there are still homes that have yet to be repaired, businesses that have never come back, people displaced, and jobs lost.

Barry Hall owns Champion Auto Service in Old North Dayton. "Our business was able to bounce back," he said. "We were without power for a few days. That's an inconvenience. It's the people in the neighborhood who are still suffering, and some jobs are gone. Grocery Lane and Frito Lay are gone for good."

Some of the players were on campus that night. Ryan Mikesell and Ibi Watson were in their apartment when Ryan's mother called to tell him that the tornadoes were coming. Coach Grant eventually called and told them to get shelter. For an East Coast native like Obi Toppin, getting an alert on his phone that a tornado was just miles away was a unique and harrowing experience.

Anthony Grant was no stranger to tornadoes. In 2011 An EF-4 tornado destroyed portions of Tuscaloosa and Birmingham, Alabama. Sixty-four people were killed. Grant had just finished his second year as the coach of the Crimson Tide. He and his staff handed out much-needed supplies in the aftermath and established a fund to help those impacted by the devastation.

Shortly after the Memorial Day tornadoes, the basketball office contacted me and asked for ways they could help. Cox Media Group was working with the Food Bank to set up locations where people could pick up essential provisions. The best way to help was to donate money to the Food Bank, and Recruiting Coordinator Andy Farrell and Trainer Mike Mulcahey joined me one afternoon in handing out food and supplies at a church in Riverside.

While the community tried to clean up and rebuild, the Flyer basketball team was trying to rebuild as well. It was an effort that encountered many obstacles. Everyone was on campus for the start of the second summer session on Monday, July 1.

"It was our first day back on campus and the first time Moo was able to play in a pickup game that Sunday," recalled Rodney Chatman. "I got switched on him and he spun to make a move on me and caught me right below the eye with his elbow. I knew it was bad right away."

It was bad, and getting worse, so he called Mulcahey, who then took him to the hospital. Chatman had broken the orbital bone in his socket. The eye was OK, but he was on the shelf for the rest of the summer. That was just the start of a cavalcade of injuries that Mulcahey had to deal with. "Run-of-the-mill stuff," he remembered. "That seems to happen here and there. The injury bug hit us pretty big. Luckily we didn't have anything that prevented someone from being able to play this season."

Jordy Tshimanga was struggling with a knee issue. "It was hard because I went through the process twice," he told me later. "I had a knee procedure when I was at Nebraska and then had to deal with the same thing here. But there is no obstacle I can't overcome. Mike Mulcahey was incredible. He is the best trainer I ever had, because he treats you as a human being first and a basketball player second."

It seemed like every time I was on campus that

summer and early fall, someone was wearing a protective boot. I jokingly asked Mulcahey if they actually only had one boot, and the players were taking turns wearing it.

Coach Grant had a full roster that he wanted to turn loose, but could not yet. "We had one day the whole summer where we had the whole team healthy together for a workout. The next time was in Hawaii," he said.

UD students were wrapping up the second summer session. Final exams were on August 9–10. On Saturday, August 3, 2019, some players went to the Oregon District in the evening. The Oregon District is one of the historical neighborhoods in Dayton. Houses are held to strict architectural standards. The neighborhood is bordered by Fifth Street, a throwback of cobblestones lined by restaurants, bars, and eclectic shops. Its proximity to the University of Dayton campus draws students as well as a mix of people from all walks of life, young and old, throughout the Miami Valley.

For many years I took guitar lessons from John Filbrun, an outstanding guitar player, who lives in Bellbrook. That Saturday he was working in his driveway when he saw a neighbor across the street wave to him as he got into a gray Toyota Corolla. That car was driven by Connor Betts who, along with his sister, drove to the Oregon District. What his motivation was that night will never be known. What he did will forever be burned into the memory of the community.

Betts, his sister, and their friend parked in a lot behind Thai 9 Restaurant and walked down an alley to enter Blind Bob's Bar shortly after 11:00 p.m. He left the other two about an hour later, and returned to his car. His sister and friend stayed a bit longer and then left. Betts changed into dark clothing, a mask, hearing protection, and body armor and was heavily armed as he walked back down the alley toward Blind Bob's. He opened fired on the patio there and upon reaching Fifth Street shot his sister and two others at a taco stand and then opened fire across the street at the crowd heading into Ned Pepper's.

Trey Landers ran into Ned Pepper's for cover and then continued out the back door, and hopped a fence. Betts never got inside Ned Pepper's, as heroic bouncer Jeremy Ganger herded customers into the door and made himself a human barricade. As Betts advanced he was stopped short. Six Dayton police officers heroically prevented further tragedy, bringing the shooter down in a hail of bullets. Ganger, who was wounded in the leg, disarmed Betts, who lay lifeless on the street. Thirty-two seconds after he fired his first shot, the Dayton police had ended the carnage, but not before nine people were killed and twenty-seven were wounded.

In addition to Landers, who escaped unharmed, Ryan Mikesell, Jordy Tshimanga, and Jhery Matos were at the taco stand getting something to eat while waiting for their Uber driver. The driver went past them, so they had to walk farther down the street to get in his car. They had nearly reached the vehicle when the shooting began. They were mere seconds removed from the spot where Betts shot his sister.

Word spread of the shootings. Players received frantic calls from family and friends, and Coach Grant, as he had on the night of the tornadoes, checked on their safety, bringing them all together on campus. Ryan Mikesell's parents were in St. Henry that evening, their phones turned off. Upon waking Sunday morning, his dad, Reed saw that he had a message from Coach Grant. While he returned that call, his wife was on the phone with Ryan.

"First thing Coach said was, 'How can I help you guys?'" Reed told me. "We took quick showers and drove down to Dayton and took Ryan and Jordy out to breakfast at Tank's. Ironically, right across the table from us was one of the surgeons from Miami Valley Hospital who had been working all night, treating the wounded."

UD grads Jeff and Leslie Gonya own Inn Port D'Vino bed and breakfast in the Oregon District. Betts most assuredly walked past their business that night down the alley toward Blind Bob's. They had met while attending the university.

"Leslie grew up in Dayton and went to Holy Angels. She had a crush on Kevin Conrad. She watched the '84 run and was hooked," Jeff told me. "I was from Fremont, Ohio, and went to Saint Joseph's High School. Of our graduating class of seventy-two, five of us went to UD. We all watched the 1990 NCAA Tournament when the Flyers beat Illinois before losing to Arkansas."

Jeff said their love of the Flyers followed them post-graduation. "After we got married we decided to get season tickets as an anniversary present to each other."

Leslie became involved in the travel business and in 2000 organized a trip for fans to attend the Maui Invitational. Every year since she has put together outings to early season exempt tournaments, various road games, and the A-10 tournament.

They were not home the night of the shooting, having just arrived at St. George Island in Florida to begin a week's vacation.

"The following morning, we started to get bombarded with Facebook messages asking if we were OK," Jeff recalled. "We saw the news and had to drive a few minutes away to get cell phone service and get in touch with people. We felt numb as we went to church that morning. When the priest found out where we were from, he asked, "Do you know anybody who was shot?"

It turned out they did not know any of those who died, but one of their favorite servers at Blind Bob's was among the wounded.

Jeff continued to remember the tragedy, "We had a full house of guests that night. Police used our parking lot as a staging ground. When we came back we had a sense of being violated. Innocence was lost in our neighborhood. In the past, we had to deal with some bar fights, drunks doing stupid stuff, but nothing like this."

I was preparing to leave for a trip to Mexico that Monday. Sunday morning, I was getting ready to go to Mass when my wife told me, "You're probably going to have to go into work. There's been a shooting in the Oregon District."

I listened to our coverage as I drove to the station. Information was trickling in, but the enormity of what happened was becoming more and more evident. I took listener phone calls while also monitoring the press conferences of Dayton Mayor Nan Whaley and Police Chief Richard Biehl. I had few answers for the listeners, but merely provided for them an opportunity to openly grieve. I had no idea that those Flyer players had been there that night, and I didn't learn about it until much later. I left for my trip on Monday, glad to put some physical distance between myself and the tragedy. It was surreal to watch TV in Mexico and see a news coverage of Dayton, Ohio. Nine lives had been lost. Dozens more had been irrevocably changed and a community, already scarred by the wrath of nature a little more than two months earlier, was again in pain.

As the Dayton Flyers tried to get through their collective sore ankles, wrists, knees, and hips, their recovery would eventually help a city and a region to heal.

UD Arena security guard Bill Myers

08

A WORK IN PROGRESS

THERE REALLY ISN'T ANY SUCH THING as an off-season anymore in college basketball. Teams are allowed to hold not just individual workouts, but whole-squad practices for a few hours at a time during the summer. In addition, the strength and conditioning coach has full reign during the summer. When Ed Streit left in early August, Casey Cathrall was quickly named to replace him, as he returned from the University of Miami (FL) to resume work with players like Obi Toppin, Trey Landers, Ryan Mikesell, and Jalen Crutcher, who were with the team when he was the strength coach in Grant's first year. The Cathrall-to-Streit-back-to-Cathrall transition appeared to be a smooth one. Those players made uninterrupted progress and Casey continued to help Jordy Tshimanga drop weight, despite dealing with a knee injury. From my perspective, the team passed the eyeball test. They looked long and strong, lean and athletic.

I talked to Ryan Mikesell about incorporating the guys who had sat out into the mix. "We've been building the chemistry," he said. "It's been really easy this summer. A lot of familiar faces still. We're excited for the games to start and for the fans to see what we've been working on."

And how good did he think this team could be? "I think the sky's the limit," he replied quickly. "Everyone on the team brings something different to the roster. The key is finding that sweet spot that each player needs in order to be impactful. If we can get everyone to be on the same page, it will be awesome."

I asked Jalen Crutcher if he could be more productive, playing fewer minutes than he did as a freshman and sophomore. "For sure," he answered. "Last year and my freshman year I would be tired toward the end of games. When you are tired and you are shooting the ball, you are more likely to miss some shots."

Full-scale practice began October 1, and Coach Grant addressed a small group of us from the media, talking about his 2019–2020 edition of the Flyers. "They really get along well together. There's a respect level they have for each other. There is a competitiveness that they enjoy, they embrace. Those are good signs. Once we get started, I think we'll be able to see where we are and what kind of jumps we need to make as we prepare for the season."

The day before, I had submitted my pre-season A-10 ballot. I picked Obi for First Team All-Conference and Jalen Crutcher for Second Team. My fellow voters agreed, with Obi joined on the First Team by Kellan Grady and Jón-Axel Guðmundsson of Davidson, Cyril Langevine of Rhode Island, Jacob Gilyard of Richmond, and VCU's Marcus Evans. Joining Jalen on the Second Team was Justin Kier from George Mason, Jeff Dowton from Rhode Island, Richmond's

Grant Golden, Kyle Lofton of St. Bonaventure, and Hasahn French from Saint Louis. Sincere Carry of Duquesne, Fatts Russell of Rhode Island, St. Bonaventure's Osun Osunniyi, Jordan Goodwin of Saint Louis, De'Riante Jenkins and Marcus Santos-Silva of VCU made up the Third Team.

We were also asked to pick the teams' order of finish. Here is what my ballot looked like:

1. Dayton
2. VCU
3. Davidson
4. Richmond
5. Saint Louis
6. Rhode Island
7. Saint Bonaventure
8. Duquesne
9. George Mason
10. UMass
11. George Washington
12. LaSalle
13. Fordham
14. Saint Joseph's

The results of the voting looked quite different.

PRESEASON POLL
(First-place votes in parentheses)

1. VCU (19)   381
2. Davidson (8)   359
3. Dayton (1)   341
4. Rhode Island   283
5. St. Bonaventure   280
6. Richmond   248
7. Saint Louis   225

8.	Duquesne	196
9.	George Mason	185
10.	La Salle	133
11.	Massachusetts	103
12.	George Washington	93
13.	Saint Joseph's	65
14.	Fordham	48

And as I already mentioned in chapter 1, I was the lone person who picked Dayton.

The Flyers tuned up for the season with an exhibition game vs. Cedarville University. I missed the game, as I broadcast the Dayton football game at Morehead State that afternoon. I listened to Tom Michaels and Keith Waleskowsi call the game on the bus ride back. Ibi Watson had 17 points in his first game in a UD uniform as the Flyers rolled to a 93–60 win. Two other new faces—Rodney Chatman and Moulaye Sissoko—had 12 points each. Moo played 20 minutes in the game, but that was the last time he saw the floor outside of warm-ups, as he opted to redshirt.

Coach Grant was upbeat in his post-game radio comments. "Defense creating offense, we had guys sharing the ball," he said. "We had 19 assists for the game. The ball moved and I think that's when we are at our best."

One week later the season began in earnest against Indiana State. The game also marked a grand reopening of sorts for the UD Arena. A three-year, $76.2 million project was complete, and the sellout crowd of 13,407 were treated to a special pre-game intro video that included legendary former Coach Don Donoher walking toward the camera and then saying, "Flyer Fans—are you ready?"

The ovation from the crowd answered that question. As the starting lineups were introduced, the floor was illuminated with the players' names. The floor had an almost cream-colored hue to it and really popped under the lights. The original construction cost of the Arena when it opened in 1969 was $4.5 million, which would be $33.9 million in 2019 dollars. The renovation was twice that amount and looked every bit of it!

The starting lineup included two of the players who had sat out the previous season. Chase Johnson and Rodney Chatman joined Obi Toppin, Jalen Crutcher, and Ryan Mikesell. Right before the national anthem, a moment of silence was held for Dayton police officer Jorge Del Rio.

John Bedell is the host of *Flyer Feedback* following Dayton basketball games and is also a reporter and anchor for WHIO-TV. He recalled how the death of Del Rio was another gut punch for the community:

> Detective Jorge Del Rio's death was hard to take because he was a man who, by all accounts, represented the best of us. He died protecting the Dayton community he loved. Del Rio was serving a drug-related search warrant with the DEA task force he served on at a house on Ruskin Road in Dayton. He was shot twice during the raid and critically injured. He died at Grandview Medical Center later that week—but not before his final act of selfless service: Jorge was an organ donor.

Del Rio was shot on Monday, November 4, 2019, and died on Thursday. That same UD Arena that stood in silence in his honor would be the site of his visitation the coming Monday and Tuesday. Arena security staff, many of whom are current or former Dayton police officers, all wore black sashes over their name badges with the number "262" in white—Jorge Del Rio's badge number.

So, it was with a wide range of emotions, excitement, anticipation, sadness, and hope that it was finally time to play basketball. Dayton won the game, but there was really nothing that night that looked to be a harbinger of greatness. It was a solid performance, but far from dominant in an 86–81 win. Trey Landers's two free throws with three seconds to play sealed the victory. Obi Toppin had a career high of 29 points as he picked up where he left off the previous season. Jalen Crutcher had 14 and Rodney Chatman, the other half of what was a unique dual point guard lineup, added 12 in his Flyers debut.

"It was always the plan that Jalen and I would play together. He was coming to Chattanooga to do that, so when he went to Dayton, it was always in the back of my mind that we could team up," Rodney told me later. "Playing with him made the game a whole lot easier. No matter what the other team did, I knew that me and Jalen could make a play."

Ryan Mikesell also scored 12 points, and Ibi Watson hit two of his four 3-point attempts in the first meaningful minutes of college basketball he had played in a long time.

Coach Grant was upbeat but not effusing praise in his post-game interview with me. "I thought it was a great atmosphere tonight, obviously a terrific crowd," he said to the radio audience and those listening on the Arena sound system. "The last twelve minutes we kind of lost our focus. They did a good job of attacking us. They got 3's, they got to the rim, they got to the foul line. That's a great opportunity for us to learn and understand what goes into winning."

Offensively, the Flyers shared the ball, notching 18 assists, and shot 48% from the field overall, but only 26% from 3-point range. Grant was not concerned about the offense, though. "I think this is a team that can have five, six, or seven guys in double figures on any given night. We have a variety of different guys who can step up."

I asked how important communicating on defense would be for this team. "That will be the whole key for us," he replied. "How good can we be from a defensive standpoint?"

What seemed to be missing in that game, from my perspective, was that the Flyers seemed to be the sum of their individual parts and not a greater whole. "This is a team, I think because we had a lot of guys miss time in the preseason, that hadn't had a lot of time to develop that chemistry," Grant agreed. "Getting to know each other and understand each other's strengths and weaknesses. Offensively and defensively, as they play together a little bit more I think this team has a chance to really grow."

That next chance to grow came a week later at home against Charleston Southern. This game was the "mainland" part of the Maui Invitational. It was the second and last game I missed due to a conflict with Flyer Football. Dayton had rallied from a 22–7 deficit to beat Drake on the road, with Fairborn's Brandon Easterling giving UD its first lead with a 100-yard interception return for a momentum-swinging touchdown. I only was able to hear the tail-end of the basketball game, and when I listened in to Tom Michaels and Brooks Hall, the bench was being emptied in a 90–61 rout. Trey Landers moved back into the starting lineup, supplanting Chase Johnson, and all five starters scored in double figures, led by Obi Toppin with 21 points and 11 rebounds. While the win was more convincing than the opener vs. Indiana State, it was not impressive, given the quality of the opponent.

Dayton would have one more challenge before going to Maui, and that came three days later against Omaha. The Mavericks had won 21 games the previous season, and had a true post player in 6'8" Matt Pile. He was no match for Obi Toppin. While Pile was held to just 8 points on 3-for-11 shooting from the field, Obi had 21 points for the second straight game. Jalen Crutcher had 7 of a team total of 21 assists, with Obi often on the receiving end.

"Crutcher, lobbing—Obi with a two-handed flush! Oh my gosh! Oh my gosh!" I said on radio.

"He was head at the rim on that one, just slid behind the defense. I don't know how you forget about a guy like Obi Toppin," chimed in Keith Waleskowski.

The final score of 93–68 was emphatic and impressive and pleasing to Coach Grant. "We got a great effort tonight from our entire roster. The five guys who started the game gave us a great effort, great energy," he told the post-game radio audience. "I thought the pace of the game was really good and when we subbed, the guys coming in off the bench continued that energy. I thought it was one of the best defensive halves of the year up to this point."

The final box score was indicative of how well Dayton played, but stats the general public does not see really told the story. "We keep what we call hustle stats," Grant continued. "And I think we set a record tonight. We had over 60 hustle stats tonight, whether it's getting a piece of the ball, a deflection, a steal, a 5-second violation, a 30-second violation. We were active tonight. We were engaged. We were connected."

Former Dayton police officer Bill Myers is one of the security officers at the Arena for basketball games. He is in charge of the visiting team, escorting the opposing coach off and on the floor safely, while keeping an eye on the crowd should anything be directed toward the opponents' bench. After the season Myers told me about a conversation with Omaha Coach Derrin Hansen after the game.

"He asked me, 'Where are you guys picked to finish in your league?'" Myers said. "I told him third, and he said, 'You're telling me there are two [bleeping] teams in the A-10 better than them!'"

Hansen proved to be a prophet, as the Flyers now prepared for the national spotlight, three games in the Maui Invitational.

"We're excited about the opportunity," said Grant on the radio. "We'll have a couple of days here to recover from tonight, and then it's Aloha!"

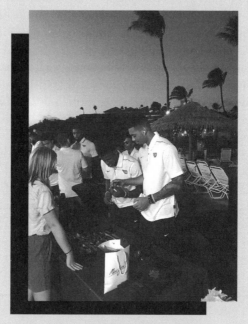

**Players get outfitted for their Maui Jim
sunglasses in Maui**

09

WOWING IN MAUI

I LOVE MY JOB. I'VE BEEN AT WHIO since March of 1981, beginning as an overnight board operator. I then was the legendary Lou Emm's producer on the morning show, and in September I replaced Chris Harris doing the daily sportscasts. The following November I succeeded him as Voice of the Flyers, a position I've held ever since, with the exception of the 1999–2000 season, when I stepped aside, having taken on the Program Director duties. I "hired" myself back the next season, and then in December of 2003 moved out of management and became the host of *Miami Valley's Morning News*. Every role has been a learning experience, a chance for personal and professional growth. The biggest highlight through the years has been the people I have met and worked with, plus I get a front-row seat at the UD Arena.

Another perk is the opportunity to travel. In my

role at WHIO Radio I have spent time in Russia, mentoring a fledgling radio station there. I have hosted listener trips to Alaska, Ireland, Italy, and Greece. And I have been to Hawaii nine times. One time was for a Cox Radio convention, another when I hosted a listener trip in the summer of 2017, and the rest with Flyer basketball.

In 1987 Dayton, under Coach Don Donoher, played in the Chaminade Christmas Classic in Honolulu. UD beat Chaminade the first game, scored 99 points on Christmas Eve vs. Oklahoma—and lost by 52—and then capped the trip with a Christmas Day defeat at the hands of LaSalle, led by future NBA player Lionel "The Train" Simmons.

In 1991 Jim O'Brien was the coach when Dayton lost to third-ranked Arizona and Montana State in the Hawaii Tip-Off tournament in Honolulu.

In Oliver Purnell's second season, Dayton split games, losing to Hawaii and beating LSU in the 1995 United Airlines Classic in Honolulu. Purnell was still the coach when the Flyers made their first appearance in the Maui Invitational in 2000. Part of a stellar field, Dayton upset 12th-ranked UConn, lost to No. 1 Arizona, and then pulled off another upset, beating 6th-ranked Maryland. What I remember most about that game was afterward, riding on the team bus as it passed Terps Coach Gary Williams walking along the highway back to the hotel. I swear he had smoke coming out of his ears.

Good things continued to happen in Maui in 2003. New Dayton coach Brian Gregory made his debut with a win at Pepperdine on the way to the island. The Flyers beat Central Michigan in the opener and anticipated a matchup with Ohio State, but the Buckeyes got beat by San Diego State. Dayton then beat the Aztecs to set up a championship matchup against the University of Hawaii. Trailing at the half by nine, Gregory decided to switch to a zone defense for the second half. The problem: Dayton had not installed a zone defense yet. Add another wrinkle to that problem: The locker rooms at the Lahaina Civic Center is actually just one room, with a curtain in the middle dividing the two teams. With the Rainbow Warriors on the other side of the curtain, the Flyer coaches whispered instructions as they walked the team through the zone defense. It worked. The zone stymied Hawaii, and Dayton's offense took over.

Keith Waleskowski remembered the comeback: "During that run, there was a broken play, and Mark Jones got himself into some trouble, almost stuck on the wing. I came and took a hand-off from him, a situation that no one would have ever drawn up, curled down the middle, and finished with a one-handed tomahawk slam. It was as thunderous as anything I was capable of, and helped keep momentum on our side to finish off the championship."

Ramod Marshall finished with 27, Keith Waleskowski had 17, and the Flyers took home the trophy (which manager Dan Helm dropped and broke) with an 82–72 final. Waleskowski was named the MVP and put his name on the banner that still hangs along with that of the Champion Flyers.

My third trip to Maui came in 2014, and wins over 10th-ranked Gonzaga and California were sandwiched around a last-second loss to No. 17 Baylor. That tournament jump started Archie Miller's Flyers, who then overcame a bad A-10 start in January to make an Elite Eight run in the NCAA Tournament.

As I prepared for my ninth trip to Hawaii, and my fourth trip to Maui under a fourth different UD Coach, I was well aware of the only downside to a trip to Paradise—getting there. Four back surgeries had my body dreading the thought of the flight, including the nearly 10-hour second leg from Denver to Maui. The week before we left, I went online and upgraded my ticket to an exit row.

An uneventful flight from Dayton to Denver saw the players forced to walk across the tarmac to the terminal in the midst of snowfall. No one seemed to mind, as it simply offered a sharp contrast to the tropical weather that awaited them. Keith Waleskowski was working the tournament with me on radio. Bucky had begged off long before the season began, and while it made sense to have Josh Postorino do the games with me, as he was going anyway as part of his duties with the University Development Office, I wanted Keith to revisit the scene of his MVP performance and to see for himself his name on the banner in the Lahaina Civic Center. In fact, Keith is the only Flyer to have played in two Maui Invitationals, as a redshirt freshman in 2000 and then as a senior in 2003.

With my upgraded boarding pass in hand, I got on the plane looking forward to catching up on some reading, or even watching a movie to pass the time pain-free. When I found my seat, I realized there was an added bonus. I was sitting next to Obi, which meant I could pick his brain for some information for the broadcast. I was just settling in when Jordy Tshimanga approached me. "Can you switch seats with me, please?" he said.

"I paid $75 extra for this," I replied.

"I will give you the $75!" he countered. "I can't even fit into the seat that's assigned."

"Jordy, I'm not going to take your money," I said and gathered up my things to sit a few rows back in a middle seat. As soon as I sat down, I realized it would have been physically impossible for him to fit his 6'11",

268-pound frame in that seat. Actually, it was OK for me, and the university reimbursed me for the money I had spent for the upgrade. While I was reading and watching movies, Jordy joined Obi to provide inflight entertainment for the rest of the plane, singing songs with kids and bantering with the flight attendants.

We arrived in the afternoon, Hawaii time, although our bodies were telling us differently. Keith and I grabbed our rental car and headed for Kaanapali and the Sheraton Black Rock Hotel. That was the same hotel the Flyers stayed at in 2003. I can remember we arrived that night just in time to see the sunset cere-mony, whereby someone in traditional island costume climbed to the top of Black Rock and threw a torch into the ocean before diving in himself. The next day I was sitting at the pool when I saw a group of tall figures walking along Black Rock. It was Waleskowski, Sean Finn, James Cripe, walk-on Jon Kingston, and manager Dan Helm. As I watched them jump in, all I could think was *We can't afford to lose two starting big men and their backup doing a crazy stunt like that!* I guess I should have had as much concern for Kingston and Helm. It's a good thing Gregory and his staff were sequestered, watching film. Keith remembered the jump: "Basically, we walked out back, saw a giant rock that looked like it would be fun to jump off of, saw some other people doing it, and joined in. Obviously, we didn't tell anyone we were going to do it before we did. Better to ask for forgiveness than permission, knowing the idea would be turned down, right?"

Keith and I talked about that and his other mem-ories of previous trips as we made the approximate-ly 45-minute drive. We were both tired when we checked in, but experience has taught me it's best to stay up and try to get on local time. We checked out the beach, had a few drinks at a poolside bar, and then joined Josh Postorino for a quick dinner in Lahaina.

Saturday was a chance to recover from the flight and to reorient at the Sheraton Black Rock Hotel. It was undergoing renovations and the main lobby was closed, as were some of the restaurants. Keith's wife, Chrissy, who also played basketball at UD, was flying in later in the afternoon. We drove to the airport to pick her up, taking a bit of detour to eat lunch at a restaurant recommended by Flyer Feedback Host John Bedell.

We drove through a rainstorm to get to the Kihei Caffe, only to discover it was closed—because of the rain! Most of the dining was outside and the tables and chairs were wet, and there was standing water on the floor. It's the only time I can ever recall a meal in a restaurant getting rained out.

After picking up Chrissy, we drove back to Kaana-pali and met with some Dayton fans who were staying at the Sheraton, including my long-time friends Bob and Marilyn Yux and Rick Kohnen. Rick is an avid fan and loyal booster but is always a "glass half-empty" type of guy when it comes to the Flyers. He was bemoaning the fact that Dayton was near the bottom of the national statistics in 3-point field goal percentage defense. First of all, I explained, a three-game sample is hardly an accurate snapshot, but also in those three games UD had limited their opponents to well under their average 3-point attempts per game. Running teams off the line is the first part of 3-point defense. We agreed to disagree, but for me it underscored that despite the progress made from the nail-biting opener to the convincing rout of Omaha, Flyer fans remained skeptical about this team.

The Maui trip is great for the fans, great for the players, a lot of work for the coaches, and great for the broadcasters, but I think no one enjoys the experience more than the managers. These UD students put in long hours and are truly invested members of the program. Four of them made this trip: seniors Henry Stark and Alex Reilly and juniors Alex Roberts and Matt Weckesser.

"That was the most fun ever," Stark told me later. "It was an amazing life experience. We were able to hang out at the beach and go snorkeling. I saw a giant sea turtle just off of Black Rock."

The guys squeezed their fun around doing laundry and setting up and helping run practice. On Saturday, the Flyers practiced at a local high school. "Coach tells us we are an extension of the coaching staff, and if we can do some of the little jobs, it allows them to focus on the larger tasks," recalled Weckesser. "One thing Coach Grant emphasized is straightening out the ball rack, so that each basketball is facing with the logo out and in a straight line. It was something he brought with him from the Thunder, and it was a way of making the gym look organized."

Weckesser came to UD after playing soccer and basketball at Chaminade-Julienne High School in Dayton. "During my freshman year I interviewed with Neil Sullivan about ways I could get involved in the athletic department," he said. "I helped out at camp the summer before my sophomore year and then I interviewed with Matt Sweet and Andy Farrell and became a manager."

Stark and Reilly both had plans of getting into coaching. "I was looking to become a grad assistant," Stark told me. "I knew I was not good enough to play Division I basketball, but I still wanted to be involved. So, I was looking for schools where I could start by being a manager. My high school coach was friends with Tom Ostrum [part of Archie Miller's staff], so I came to Dayton."

"I was a manager for three sports in high school and I wanted to get into coaching, specifically basketball," Alex Reilly explained. "My freshman year was with Coach Miller. I was asleep on a Saturday morning and my roommate woke me up and said 'Archie's gone!' He and the other managers who stayed on didn't know what to expect but noticed some differences right away during the transition. I was helping out as Coach Grant was working out the big men," Reilly said. "Afterwards he played them one-on-one. I was impressed."

Sunday began the big buildup for the tournament. All the coaches and some select players attended a press conference down the beach at the Hyatt. Jay Bilas did a "94-feet" interview with Obi, walking along the sand. Keith and I spent time talking to Bilas and play-by-play announcer Dan Shulman, as they picked our brains about the Flyers. One of the ESPN producers joined us and said he was impressed, again, at the large following of UD fans there in Maui. Shulman was the emcee of the press conference featuring all eight coaches. Joining Anthony Grant was Tom Crean, coach of the Flyers' first-round opponent Georgia, Mike Young of Virginia Tech, Tom Izzo of Michigan State, Mark Pope from BYU, Kansas's Bill Self, Mick Cronin of UCLA, and Eric Bovaird of Chaminade. I can paraphrase what every coach said: "We are honored to be here. This is a tremendous field. We are not very good right now, but we are hoping to get better."

Coach Grant spent some time expounding on what a privilege he felt it was to be coaching at his alma mater and warned the other coaches that the Flyer Faithful would be making their presence felt in the tiny Lahaina Civic Center Gym. After the press conference, Keith and I joined Coach Grant as Sports

Information Director Doug Hauschild drove us all to practice at said gym. Keith got to see his name up on the MVP banner and the banner displaying the Flyers as 2003 champs. "It was an awesome feeling to be back in that gym again! I was humbled and proud to see my name in person up there with so many greats on the MVP banner, as well as our team on the past champions banner," said Waleskowski. "There were many congratulations to go around and it was great to reminisce with some of the current players and staff." There were also some banners outside depicting past participants in the event, including Grad Assistant Khyle Marshall in his Butler-playing days.

This was not a practice in which we would pick up a lot of scouting report information. It was a chance for the players to get familiar with the floor and the rims, and also for the ESPN crews to get familiar with Dayton personnel. It was also my first Bill Walton experience.

Bill Walton's connection to Dayton Flyer basket-ball began when he was a player. As a senior at UCLA he participated in one of the most famous games in the history of UD basketball. Ironically, it was a loss, as Dayton fell to the Bruins 111–100 in triple over-time in the regional semis of the 1974 NCAA Tour-nament. After college Walton enjoyed a 14-year NBA career, winning championship rings with Portland in 1977 (where he was a teammate of Flyer great Johnny Davis) and in Boston in 1986. Throughout his career he was known as a free spirit. He is a Dead Head, having attended 850 Grateful Dead concerts through the years, and along the way he *may* have partaken in something that is legal for medical use in many states and for recreational use, as well, in a few more.

I missed hearing him speak in Dayton at the Ag-onis Club a few years back but heard it was quite the unique presentation. I had also watched games he had worked for ESPN as a color analyst. If you had no real interest in the teams involved or the outcome, he was very entertaining. If you were trying to follow the game, he was frustrating.

Shortly after Keith and I arrived, Walton approached me. "Hi, I'm Bill," he said, extending his hand, "what's your name?" I told him and then he asked what my involvement was with the program. He picked my brain for several minutes, asking questions about the players, coaches, even going so far as to have me identify some of the coaches' sons who were there. All that information was scribbled on a stack of papers in such a manner that only he knew how to retrieve it later. After he was finished, he pointed at me and said: "You're Larry. I'm Bill," and then he left to repeat the same procedure with everyone else in the gym. He spent a lot of time talking with Keith and Ricardo Greer, once I told him that Ricardo had been inducted into the French Basketball Hall of Fame. Walton introduced himself to all of the players, who probably only thought of him as an old guy with scarred knees and support stockings for whom every step was painful, and not one of the greatest college basketball players of all time.

Walton was done and practice was over. As the players were changing shoes, Anthony's sons, A. J. (Anthony Jr.) and Makai, along with Ricardo Greer's son R. J. (Ricardo Jr.), were out on the court shooting around. Suddenly, there was a roar from the players and Coach Grant broke into the biggest smile I had ever seen. Anthony is not a stoic person, but usually maintains an even keel. He can make a player's knees buckle with a withering glare after a mistake is made, and once games are well in hand he will allow fans to see him grin along the sidelines. However, this smile was not that of a basketball coach. This was the smile of a proud parent. His youngest son, Makai, who was in middle school, had just dunked for the first time.

Between the press conference and a fun practice, it was an upbeat day overall but still did not ease the mounting tension that everyone in the program felt, as well as fans there in Maui and back home. Dayton would be facing its first quality opponent the next day in the Georgia Bulldogs out of the SEC. The first game in these three-game early season tournaments is the largest hurdle. Win that game, and there is a palpable sense of relief with the realization that the team is not going to come away completely empty. Plus, a win in game one usually means a chance to play a better opponent in game two. The buildup for the Georgia game was not just about trying to get a win over an SEC team but also the anticipation of a meeting with Michigan State in the second game. The Spartans had been the No.1 team in the Associated Press preseason poll.

I capped off that Sunday night before the Georgia game by attending the Old Lahaina Luau with Keith and Chrissy, as well as my friends Bob and Mary Lynn Yux, Rick Kohnen, and Kathy Sturm. The food was great, and the show was spectacular, but the business part of the trip was about to begin.

Obi was already receiving a lot of national attention when we arrived in Maui, but he was somewhat overshadowed by Georgia freshman Anthony Edwards. A 6'5" guard, Edwards was expected to play just one year with the Bulldogs and then become a lottery pick in the NBA draft. He scored 24 points in his collegiate debut against Western Carolina, 29 in a win over the Citadel, had just 6 points but 7 assists in a win over Delaware State, and then bounced back with an 18-point performance vs. Georgia Tech. Like Dayton, Georgia was undefeated but had played one more game, and with the ACC opponent Georgia Tech, had played a better schedule.

The Flyers and Bulldogs were the first game to begin the tournament, tipping off at 2:30 p.m. EST, which was 9:30 a.m. local time in Maui. The Flyer Faithful were undeterred by the early start, and bars in Lahaina accommodated them by opening early for pre-game festivities.

While fans were making their presence felt at watering holes, the Flyers gave them plenty to cheer about right away when they got to the Lahaina Civic Center. A 14–2 run was sparked by a perfect 6-for-6 from the field from Obi Toppin. Dayton led by 18 at the half and never looked back, rolling to an 80–61 rout of the Bulldogs. Obi led the way with 25, and his best friend and roommate Jalen Crutcher had 20, including a three at the buzzer to end the first half. Edwards, Georgia's heralded freshman, was held to just 6 points on 2-for-10 shooting from the field and missed all 5 of his 3-point attempts. Dayton was able to play everybody, as Jordy Tshimanga saw his first action coming off the knee injury that had plagued him since the summer.

Afterward Coach Grant talked with me on WHIO Radio. "I thought our guys did a really good job of understanding the scouting report," he said. "We were locked in from a defensive standpoint and our defensive focus helped fuel us, and we got some easy baskets."

I remarked, "How important was it that when guys came into the game, they just did their job?" "There you go," Grant quickly responded. "That's the whole key. In a nutshell, that's what we're looking for."

Keith, Chrissy, and I went to lunch after the game

in Lahaina, where we didn't see a lot of Dayton fans walking around. We watched the Michigan State–Virginia Tech game on TV, and the Hokies pulled off a 71–66 upset of the No. 3 Spartans. Dayton was not going to get the marquee matchup they had hoped for the next day, but fans were buzzing about the Flyers' performance when we got back to the hotel. That night Sports Information Director Doug Hauschild called and asked me for a favor. The tournament had hired podcasters Titus & Tate to be their social media correspondents, and they were doing a wrap-up of each day on YouTube from the Arena after all the games were over. Doug's son, Michael, was proposing to his fiancée that night on the beach, so Doug needed to be with his family. He wanted me to drive Obi over to the Lahaina Civic Center so he could be interviewed. The Flyers were just finishing their meal in the team room when I approached Coach Grant and asked him if I could take Obi to the gym. He looked at me as if I had three eyes! "OK by me," I said. "One less thing I have to do." And I left to join friends at the poolside bar.

After playing at 9:30 in the morning on Monday, it seemed like an eternity waiting for the 3:00 p.m. local time start against Virginia Tech. I watched the earlier losers' bracket games between Michigan State and Georgia and UCLA vs. Chaminade, which meant I got to listen to Bill Walton working the games with Dave Pasch. Several times Pasch would interrupt a Walton train-of-thought soliloquy with a reminder, "There is a game going on."

Once again, the Flyer Faithful showed up in full voice, and once again they were not disappointed. After a back-and-forth start, Dayton went on a 10–0 run to open up daylight. Obi Toppin hit three straight 3's late in the half and was looking for a fourth. Here's what it sounded like on radio: "Obi fakes a pass, takes a 3, no good." And then Keith is howling as I continue, "A follow-up jam by Ibi Watson and that is how the half comes to a close!"

For the second game in a row, Dayton led by 18 at the half and again did not let up, rolling to an 89–72 victory. Dayton had 10 dunks as a team in the game, including the 100th of Obi's career. Trey Landers threw one down with authority: "Chatman penetrates and gives it to Landers," I said on the air. "Landers a tomahawk jam and a foul!" Keith jumped in, "and a flex. A flex for the camera and the fans." Chase Johnson got in on the act thanks to a no-look pass from walk-on Christian Wilson.

"The pass I made to Chase in Maui was something I've done a lot in practice," Christian told me later. "Every time I come off a ball screen, I'm looking for the big man rolling. When I came off the screen, I saw that the paint was wide open, so it was an easy pass. I put a little extra flavor with a no-look pass. I also did a little celebration running down the court because I was just so excited to be playing in Maui on national television. I went to the Bahamas last year and didn't play at all, so being able to play in Maui was a dream come true."

The Flyers were in the championship game of the Maui Invitational, awaiting the winner of Kansas and BYU. The 4th-ranked Jayhawks took care of business. Perhaps the folks at ESPN had been hoping for a Kansas vs. Michigan State final before the tournament began, but a matchup between a college basketball blue-blood and a team that was capturing the hearts of a nation was going to make for good TV.

The game started at noon local time, which gave me enough time in the morning to get a run in, have breakfast with Keith and Chrissy, and then watch a little bit of the fifth-place game between Michigan State and UCLA. In the first half, Walton was off on a tangent talking about Nigeria and asked Pasch if he had ever been there. Pasch said no, only to have Walton again ask him in early in the second half. "I told you in the first half I had never been there," said a flustered Pasch. "Well, you had all of halftime to change that," Walton replied in vintage "Hi, I'm Bill!" style.

The game against Kansas was the first one in which the Flyer Faithful did not dominate the crowd. Yes, there were more Dayton fans, but just slightly more. The game was a matchup between two of the premier big men in the nation—Obi Toppin and the Jayhawks' Udoka Azubuike—and two of the best point guards in the country—Jalen Crutcher and Devon Dotson. Rodney Chatman got in early foul trouble, but Ibi Watson came off the bench and scored 11 points in the first half. Obi made the highlight reel with a step-back corner 3, staring down the Kansas bench as the ball went through the net, and Dayton enjoyed a slim 1-point halftime lead.

The second half stayed tight, but then Crutcher hit two 3's and Watson added another to open up an 8-point Flyer lead, only to have Kansas respond with an 8–0 run. With three seconds left in the game, Dayton was trailing by 3. Here's the call on WHIO Radio: "Crutcher steps back. Crutcher lets fly a 3. Good if it goes . . . and it does with one second to go!" Keith is hollering, I'm yelling, the crowd is going crazy, and the game is going to overtime. Ryan Mikesell gave the Flyers a lift, scoring Dayton's first 7 points in the extra period, but Azubuike answered with 7 for KU, and Dotson sealed the game at the free throw line. The Flyers lost for the first time, falling 90–84. After the game Coach Grant was looking at the big picture.

"We got six games under our belt," he told me in his post-game radio interview. "We're not a finished product yet. Obviously, we'll go back and we'll learn what we can from this tournament. It was great competition. I thought we took steps in the right direction, now it's the process of getting ready for the next one. We're only six games in, so there is no finality. It's all a process."

I imagine the mood back at the hotel among fans and players would have rivaled New Year's Eve had Dayton won, but as it was, there was no sense of disappointment on anyone's part. Sure, it would have been great to be the Maui Invitational Champs, but the way this team came together, there were plenty of reasons to be optimistic. We gathered with some fans around one of the pool bars and had some dinner. Coach Grant and his wife walked across the lawn heading for the beach, and he received a standing ovation from those in the bar.

The next day was Thanksgiving. We skipped the traditional turkey dinner and Keith, Chrissy, and I went into Lahaina for a Loco Moco breakfast, consisting of a ground beef patty, sautéed onions, a sunny-side-up egg, and brown gravy served over white rice. I got some beach time in after that and ran into some of the players trying to teach Dwayne Cohill how to swim. Their success on the court that week was far greater. "I already knew how to swim," said Dwayne. "The guys were just trying help me be able to do some stuff I wanted to do." We all saw plenty of sea turtles in the water just below Black Rock. Speaking of Black Rock, did Waleskowski jump again? "You bet I did, and it was just as fun!" he told me later. "I'm still a kid at heart and can't let the old man in yet!"

By mid-afternoon it was time to check out, turn in the rental car, and begin the long flight back. Once again, Jordy and Obi provided the in-flight entertainment. Jordy was wearing a maroon velour jumpsuit, but it was a look that he, and he alone, could pull off. "Some people do it to put on a show," he explained. "But it comes natural to me. I have positive energy all the time, and I like seeing people smile."

There were plenty of reasons for Dayton players, Dayton coaches, Dayton fans, and Dayton broadcasters to smile.

**Young fan Toby Casserta at the movies
with Trey Landers, Dwyane Cohill,
Ibi Watson,Jalen Crutcher, Obi Toppin,
Jordy Tshiminga, and Jheri Matos**

10

THIS TEAM IS FOR REAL

THE 2000–2001 DAYTON TEAM THAT beat UConn and Maryland in Maui never recaptured that magic, dropping back-to-back games to Cincinnati and Marshall upon returning to the mainland and finishing a middle-of-the-pack 9–7 in the A-10, eventually losing to Detroit in the NIT quarterfinals. After winning the Maui Invitational in 2003, the Flyers kept on winning before suffering their first loss at UC in late December. That UD team won the A-10 West Division and went to the NCAA Tournament, losing to DePaul in double overtime. The 2013–2014 Flyers jump-started their season with a strong Maui performance en route to the Elite Eight of the NCAA Tournament, but it had its struggles in December and certainly January, when it started the A-10 with a 1–5 record.

With that history, there was no guarantee that the euphoria of the three games in Maui would translate into continued success. Even the giddiest of Dayton fans was waiting for the bubble to burst. Scheduling can help with the transition from the long trip to and from Hawaii back to reality in the soon-to-be-frozen Midwest. Dayton struggles to get non-conference home games, because, realistically teams don't want to schedule games they think they are going to lose. The scheduling philosophy in recent years is to try and get home-and-home series with teams from the Power Five conferences, and if not, to at least get neutral-site games. After that Dayton fills in the home schedule with "buy" games, whereby a school is paid to come to the UD Arena. Schools can earn anywhere from $50,000 to $100,000 per game. Last year Kentucky lost at home to Evansville, and the Aces cashed a $90,000 check on top of that. Teams from the SWAC will make a northern tour in November and December, playing the likes of Dayton, Ohio State, Kentucky, Louisville, Cincinnati, Xavier, and Indiana all on the same trip. One school even went so far as to put a picture of their bus driver in their media guide. A school like Texas Southern didn't play a home game before their conference season began and was able to fund their program for the entire year, win their conference tournament, and still make the NCAA Tournament, even if it was a trip to the First Four.

Dayton tries to schedule "buy" games that have a chance of helping or at least not hurting their RPI (Ratings Percentage Index) or now, their NET (NCAA Evaluation Tool). Calls are made to schools who are coming off good seasons, returning enough players to be projected to compete in their respective leagues. There are situations, however, when the intent is to schedule, realistically, a bad team: the first game after an early season exempt tournament and the last game before Christmas.

The Flyers returned from Maui with a 5–1 record and had the weekend to recover before hosting Houston Baptist on Tuesday, December 3, 2019, and then heading back out on the road for a neutral-site game in Phoenix that Sunday vs. Saint Mary's. On Monday, Dayton broke into the Associated Press Top 25 at No. 19 and were No. 17 in the coaches' poll. Houston Baptist came into the game winless and left winless. The Flyers turned a 7-point halftime lead into a 99–68 rout. All five walk-ons got in the game, with Jarod Becker scoring the game's final basket on a baseline drive and dunk. Chase Johnson came off the bench to score a career-high 18 points, having scored just 21 points total in the previous six games. Johnson had arrived on campus the previous year and enrolled in the second semester, transferring from Florida after a year and a half. He received a waiver to be eligible in the first semester this season after being plagued by concussions during his time in Gainesville.

After the game, Coach Grant was ready to move on, as he told our radio listeners. "This is a game right now the guys need to flush. Clear their minds," he said. "There's a lot that's happened over the past week for our basketball team. We have a couple of days to get prepared for a very challenging game out in Phoenix. We'll turn the page here and try to get ready for our game out there."

While Coach Grant may have not been overly impressed with his Flyers, Houston Baptist Coach Ron Contrell was. "That's a top-three team in the nation right there," he told security guard Bill Myers after the game.

The Houston Baptist coach was not the only person taking notice of the Flyers. Sports Information Director Doug Hauschild saw the respect grow among national media. "Maui is the gold standard. Once the team performed well there, they had the nation's attention, but even then, it was with a qualifier, not being in a Power 5 conference," Doug told me. "However, some of the guys at the top like Jay Bilas and Scott Van Pelt, they just took us for being good, period."

Getting the game with Saint Mary's was a challenge for Athletic Director Neil Sullivan. The Jerry Colangelo Classic was held at the Phoenix Suns' home arena, and the Flyers-Gaels matchup was the second of three games that day. Saint Louis played Tulane in the first, with Grand Canyon taking on Liberty. It took a bit of arm twisting to get Saint Mary's to consent, and then Sullivan had to deal with the powers that be at his own university. The game was scheduled on the Sunday before finals week, and Sullivan needed the permission of the faculty board in order to take the team on the road. He was able to get the green light by sending three academic advisors on the trip as well.

The charter flight arrived in Phoenix on Friday night, and I was able to meet Josh Postorino for a late dinner. Josh, who had played and coached at Dayton, had returned to his alma mater after coaching stints at Clemson, DePaul, and Georgia Tech. He worked in Development for the Athletic Department and was part of the trio of former players including Brooks Hall and Keith Waleskowski who filled in when Bucky was not able to do games. That summer he had opted to move to the Phoenix area but was still working for UD in Development, meeting with donors all over the country. It only made sense for him to work the game there in Phoenix.

Saturday was a chance for the team to practice at the Sun's arena, and it was my first taste of what would become the phenomena surrounding Obi Toppin.

While the Flyers worked out, scouts from three different NBA teams were watching, including Bubba Burrage, the Director of Player Personnel for the Suns. He sat beside me and picked my brain about Obi while asking about some of the other players as well. "What can you tell me about the big white guy in the post?" he asked, pointing to Graduate Assistant Sean Damaska, thinking he might be a player. "He's a former tight end," I replied. Damaska was in his second year on the staff. "I had been working as a player development assistant with the NBA's Dallas Mavericks and was looking for a college grad assistant job," he told me. "I had interviewed at Michigan State on a Wednesday, and they said they would get back to me on the following Monday. That Monday I didn't hear from them. Mavs assistant Mike Weiner knew Darren Hertz, and he called Darren the next day. I interviewed at Dayton and was offered the job on the spot. I accepted, even after Michigan State called back and finally made an offer. I couldn't be happier."

I told Bubba Burrage that Damaska was a tight end, because he was at Indiana. "I was a basketball player in high school [in Georgia]," he said. "I went to IU planning on being just a regular college student, but when my sister started playing soccer at Georgetown, I didn't want to be the only person in my family not playing Division I sports. I decided to walk on the football team and eventually got a scholarship." After his Hoosier football days ended, Damaska played a year of basketball as a grad transfer at Northern Illinois, and after a year with the NBA Mavs, came to Dayton. That first year was spent in on-court player development, which meant banging with Obi in practice each day. "This past season he was noticeably stronger," Damaska recalled. "He didn't look lots bigger, but he used his body well and was able to move me and everybody around.

I thought he had a chance of playing in the NBA last year, but after Maui I knew he could not only play in the NBA but be a good player for a long time."

When we returned to the hotel, there was a surprise waiting for Anthony Grant—his wife, Chris. She had flown in that morning, and just a few of us knew she was coming. When he spotted her in the lobby, he broke into a grin that rivaled the one when he saw Makai dunk for the first time in Maui. Anthony Grant the player; Anthony Grant the coach; Anthony Grant the father; Anthony Grant the husband: I've been privileged to be a witness to them all.

The Big Ten Football Championship game was that night. Friends from Dayton, including Eric Eichner and former Wright State basketball player Tom Holzapfel were in Phoenix, and I watched the game and had dinner with them and their wives. We talked basketball while watching football, and they were starting to feel like this Flyers squad could be special.

The next day I met Josh at the Arena after he attended a boosters' event. The Flyers Faithful were out in force yet again! Our broadcast position was halfway up the lower seating bowl, and we were alongside Saint Louis broadcasters Bob Ramsey and Earl Austin Jr. I have known those guys for over thirty years, and while the schools for which we broadcast may be rivals, we are all good friends. I watched the end of the first half and start of the second half of their game against Tulane and noted a freshman guard, Gibson Jimerson, knocking down threes. Long-range shooting had been the Billikens' weakness the past year, and I made a mental note that they could be a force to reckon with in the A-10.

The Flyers beat Saint Mary's 78–68, but the game was really not that close. After trailing 4–3 early, the Flyers started a 10–0 run and never looked back. Jalen Crutcher was magnificent, with 21 points and 6 assists. Obi, Trey Landers, and Ibi Watson also scored in double figures, while Rodney Chatman kept the Gaels' leading scorer, Jordan Ford, in check. Ford came into the game averaging 20.2 points per game but was held to just 11. "He was key for us," said Coach Grant on his post-game radio interview. "We knew how much they relied on him from an offensive standpoint. Not only his ability to score, but his ability to create and get the ball to guys for open 3's." He then went on to salute the Flyer Faithful. "Unbelievable, to come out and see so many people wearing Flyer Red in the stands. We have the best fans in the country."

Those fans were now even more stoked as the following day Dayton rose to 14th in the AP poll and 12th in the coaches' poll. Every Monday night during the season, unless there is a game or the team is traveling, WHIO hosts the *Anthony Grant Show* at a sports bar, Fricker's, on Woodman Drive in Dayton. There is a back room set aside for the show, and as the Flyers climbed the polls the crowds kept getting larger. On that Monday, Director of Basketball Operations James Haring came to the show along with Strength and Conditioning Coach Casey Cathrall. Haring recalled stepping up to the Bud Light mic. "I asked a question that I basically already knew the answer to," he said. "And that was what were Coach's favorite beverages. I knew it was Perrier and then his afternoon latté." A few days later Grant was on the *Jim Rome Radio Show*, and Rome hit him with a final question, "What's your favorite latté?" Anthony replied, "Either a vanilla or a chai tea latté, and lately it's been the chai tea." Sports Information Director Doug Hauschild told me Rome's producers got that info from a link to the radio show from the Dayton Basketball Twitter feed.

Final exam week was largely uneventful, with the

Flyers returning to action that Saturday at home against Drake. Before each home game I would go back into the coaches' locker room area ninety minutes before tip-off and record the pre-game interview with Anthony. Before we started, he told me that Chase Johnson would not be in uniform that night. "Illness," was his response to my raised eyebrow. Even with Dayton a man down, the Bulldogs were no match for the 14th-ranked Flyers. Ibi Watson came off the bench to score a career-high 20 points as Dayton turned a 12-point halftime lead into a 78–47 drubbing. Once he got to Maui, Watson had found his game legs and rhythm. His release is so pure, with perfect arc and a soft touch, I am surprised when the ball does not go in. "Ibi. Open. Three. Good," became a mantra for me on the radio.

That Monday the Flyers remained 12th in the coaches' poll but moved up to 13th in the AP. Another test was awaiting them that Saturday vs. Colorado in the Chicago Legends doubleheader at the United Center in Chicago. But North Texas was first on Tuesday and had trap game written all over it. However, the maturity of this Dayton team rose to the surface again. How many times through the years have we seen talented Flyer squads look very ordinary against an inferior-talented team? This team was not like that, and a game against the Mean Green out of Conference USA that had the Dayton coaches worried turned into win number nine on the season, as Dayton never trailed in a 71–58 victory with Jalen Crutcher and Ryan Mikesell leading the way with 16 points each.

Now the full focus could be on the rematch of last season's NIT matchup with the Buffaloes, who were again being led by Tyler Bey and the former Flyer commitment McKinley Wright. Dayton vs. Colorado was the first game of the Chicago Legends doubleheader in the United Center, with Cincinnati and Iowa playing in the nightcap. Each team was represented by a "legend," with Roosevelt Chapman on hand for the Flyers. Chapman is Dayton's all-time leading scorer and the most popular player in Flyer history. (Although Obi Toppin may have eclipsed him. More on that later.) He was also a former teammate of Anthony Grant and spoke to the team right after breakfast on game day. Josh Postorino was visiting boosters in Chicago, so he was working the game on radio with me. The night before, we had dinner with Jack Dybis, a former quarterback on UD's 1989 Division III National Championship football team, currently an ER physician in Chicago and a fan and supporter of all things involving his alma mater.

As expected, the Flyer Faithful were out in force in the United Center, far outnumbering those of Colorado, Iowa, or UC. Our broadcast position was the same as it had been in 2016 when the Flyers lost to Northwestern, at the end of the court about halfway up the first section. It was not a good vantage point, but even so I can attest that it was one of the worst-officiated games I have ever witnessed. I am reticent to complain about officiating on the air, because it can color a broadcast to the point that the fan does not know what is going on. My job is to describe what happens, not to offer a critique of the referees. However, on this occasion I needed to address it in order to describe what was going on. Even Terry Nelson, who was working the UC radio broadcast with Mo Egger, said to me after the game, "You guys didn't get a very good whistle."

That being said, the game began well for the Flyers, jumping out to a 19–5 lead, but then Colorado responded with their own 14–2 run sparked by McKinley Wright who was booed loudly by the Dayton fans every time he touched the ball. This aggravated me on two levels. Why boo a kid who felt abandoned by a coaching change and wanted to reassess his future? And secondly, why motivate a great player? Still Dayton was able to hold the lead at the half, 36–32. Colorado came out in the second half and tied the game up at the 15-minute mark and grew that lead to 7 on a pair of McKinley Wright free throws with 6:21 to go. With just under 2 minutes to play, Obi dunked to cut the Buffalo lead to 1. Evan Battey increased the Colorado lead to 2, making one of two free throws with 35 seconds to play. Obi then missed a 3 for the lead, and Dayton was forced to foul. Wright missed the front end of a two-shot foul and made the second to take Colorado back up by 3 with 13 seconds to play. Jalen Crutcher brought the ball up and passed to Obi at the top of the key. Crutcher then cut to the right wing, looking to get the ball right back, but Colorado anticipated that and denied him the ball. Obi, who had missed all five 3-point attempts so far, had no choice but to let it fly. It was good with 6 seconds to play. Wright's desperation 3 was off the mark and for the second time in the season, Dayton was headed to overtime.

The Flyers drew first blood in the overtime, and a back-and-forth battle ensued. Neither team could open any daylight. D'Shawn Schwartz hit a short jumper to give Colorado a 1-point edge with 27 seconds to play. Dayton called a time-out and Jalen Crutcher added to his "Clutcher" reputation with what looked to be a game-winning floater in the lane with 10 seconds to go. But the Flyers got their hearts broken. Colorado pushed the ball and threw it in the post to Tyler Bey. Dayton had him well defended and he kicked it out to a wide-open Schwartz who hit a 3 to give Colorado a 78–76 win.

Now I would like to revisit my previous remarks on the officiating. The reason Schwartz was wide open is that Rodney Chatman was hit by a moving screen that was actually more of a tackle. Beyond the subjective analysis, the objective numbers show that Colorado shot 21 free throws in the game compared to Dayton's 7. The Buffaloes also had 17 offensive rebounds. Give them credit, give Dayton some blame, but for them to be that physical without fouling I found hard to swallow.

The OT loss to Kansas had been disappointing, but this felt devastating. The euphoria of Crutcher's big play was wiped out by the image of Chatman lying helplessly on the floor as Schwartz's shot went through the net. Right before Josh and I went on the air, I got a call from my daughter Lauren's boyfriend, Nate Murray. They live in Cleveland, where she is the Director of the Dunham Tavern Museum and he is co-owner of Super Electric, a pinball parlor in the Gordon Square neighborhood on the west side. I did not answer, and shortly thereafter he texted, saying: "I need to talk to you." As I wallowed in my grief I nearly forgot about the text. I had some time before Anthony came up for the post-game radio interview, so I called Nate back. He wanted my blessing, as he intended to ask Lauren to marry him the next day. "You just made my day," I told him. "I was feeling lower than low, but I could not be happier now." I still wish Dayton had won the game, but I received some much-needed perspective in that moment.

When Coach Grant finally made it up to our broadcast location, he said nothing about the officiating, praised Colorado, and said his team did not play well enough to win, citing four turnovers to begin the second half. "When you give a team as good as Colorado that many opportunities . . ." he continued. "Seventeen offensive rebounds they were able to come up with. That's just a recipe for something that happened at the end. I'm not trying to take anything away from them, but some of the stuff we'll go back and look at, and before I see it, in my opinion, could have been the difference in a one- or two-possession game."

It was a quiet flight back to Dayton—what would be the second quietest of the season, with the other somber for an entirely different reason.

Chase Johnson had missed his third straight game due to an undisclosed illness and was not available again two days later at home against Grambling. Jalen Crutcher was also held out because of concussion symptoms after taking a nasty fall in the Colorado game. Ibi Watson started in his place and scored a new career-high 30 points, including a perfect 10-for-10 from the line. After playing sparingly his sophomore year at Michigan and then sitting out the transfer year, it took a while for Ibi to feel completely comfortable back on the floor. "After Maui I felt like I was back," he later told me. "It was my first meaningful basketball in two years." I was impressed how he showed such patience upon coming in off the bench, getting a feel for the game, and how he could make an impact. "I understood that we had so many guys who could score," he explained. "I just needed to be in the flow of the offense, and if I was open late in the shot-clock, I knew I could make the shot." He took just 12 shots in the game, making 8 from the field to go along with those 10 free throws. The Flyers rolled to an 81–53 win and headed into the Christmas break with a 10–2 record.

The Flyers returned to campus on December 26 to get what is traditionally the worst practice of the year out of the way, and then began preparation for their final non-conference game against North Florida. This game was Dayton at its dominating and entertaining best. In defeathering the Ospreys 77–59, Obi Toppin scored a career-high 31 points and broke his own previous school record of dunks in a game (8 vs. Detroit Mercy in 2018) with 10—team UD set a school record with 13 dunks. In addition to Obi's 10, Trey Landers had 1 and Ryan Mikesell had 2, going coast-to-coast as heard on radio. "Rebound controlled by Ryan Mikesell. Ryan did a good job of battling, and then dunks it at the other end," I said. "Ryan Mikesell," chimed in Brooks Hall. "He did a great job of battling at the other end, pushed it, kept his head up, and made the decision to keep it and finished with a two-hand dunk."

After the game in an interview with Tom Archdeacon of the *Dayton Daily News*, North Florida Coach Matt Driscoll was effusive in his praise for Obi Toppin. "I told him I was proud of the way he carries himself," Driscoll told Archdeacon. "He's such a star, but he's so unselfish, so willing to be a team guy. And it echoes more with the other guys. It gives them a confidence that they don't have to rest on quote-unquote 'one dude.' When your best dude is also your hardest worker, a great defender and with the way he shares the sugar, it affects the whole team and next thing you know they're super connected. The thing that separates this year's team from last year's is that they're not only older and more experienced, but what happened in Maui with them has a complete correlation to when they walk on the floor now. They are an extremely, extremely confident group of young men. They're borderline arrogant, but they are not arrogant, they're just confident in what they do and the way in which they do it."

A confident, energetic, athletic, personable, and coachable team was 11–2 after non-conference play, but skepticism remained in the former of the A-10 season, and a visit to the scene of a previous Dayton basketball crime—Philadelphia.

**Bill Walton talks to Jordy Tshimanga at
practice in Maui**

11

EXORCISING SOME DEMONS

IN THIRTY-EIGHT SEASONS BEHIND THE microphone for Dayton Flyers basketball, I have only a few fond memories from visits to Philadelphia. In 1984, Don Donoher took a 6–6 UD squad into a game at Temple, decided to go small, inserting Damon Goodwin in the starting lineup, and a 63–62 win jump-started a run to the Elite Eight in the NCAA Tournament. In 2009, Marcus Johnson followed up a Chris Wright missed shot with a dunk with just one second remaining for a 63–61 win at La Salle. In Archie Miller's first season the Flyers pulled off an upset at Temple, winning 87–77. What I remember most about that game, however, was Owls coach Fran Dunphy, in a classy move, calling the hotel after the game to check on the status of Luke Fabrizius, who had broken his nose.

Most of my memories of Philadelphia are of cheesesteaks instead of Dayton success, and even the cheesesteak memories are marred by most of the team getting food poisoning after a loss at Saint Joseph's in 2010. Losses at Temple (when they were in the A-10) and Saint Joseph's were somewhat tolerable, because they usually had strong teams. However, La Salle has been where the dreams of more talented Flyer teams have gone to fade away.

Part of the reason, in my opinion, is the Tom Gola Arena–Aquatic Center–Tire Service & Hair Care Salon. Actually, the name is just Tom Gola Arena, but there is a pool in the basement, and it is a multiple-use facility. When you walk into the building, you are hit with the strong chlorine odor from the pool; walk up two flights of steps and you are greeted by a hand-written note on the door saying that intramurals are canceled due to a varsity sports event. It is not as good as a typical high school gym, and the whole atmosphere has a Saturday morning rec league vibe. I can see where visiting players need to be reminded that it is a real game and it actually counts.

Dayton headed into the start of A-10 play as No. 20 in the AP poll and No. 18 in the coaches' poll. They faced what looked like a huge potential pitfall to start things off—at La Salle on Thursday, January 2, 2020, and at Saint Joseph's on Sunday, January 5. Traveling on New Year's Day, the team went directly to the "arena" to get some shots up and to help those players who had never been there to not be shocked to see what awaited them on game day. After practice, we checked into the Marriott on Market Street, which would be our home away from home for the next four nights. With the university still on break before the next semester began, there was no need to return to campus between games. Chase Johnson was still not with the team, and there was no comment from the coaches or training staff about his absence.

The next day there was a good-sized contingent of Flyer Faithful on hand and a typically small group of La Salle supporters. The problem for Dayton teams in the past has not been a hostile crowd, but rather the lack of a crowd or any type of energy in the building. When the Flyers began the game with two straight turnovers, I thought, "here we go again." But then cream began to rise to the top. La Salle had no match for Obi Toppin inside, and the Dayton defense was smothering. Sixteen La Salle turnovers led to 29 UD points and a 22-point halftime lead into an 84–58 victory. Obi led the way with 20 points and 7 rebounds with a large number of NBA scouts at the game.

The attention Obi was getting had grown exponentially. NBA scouts are always in abundance at the Maui Invitational. First, because they can see multiple players at just one place over a few days, and second, because they get a free trip to Hawaii. Scouts would also show up for games at the UD Arena. In addition to the scouts at the La Salle game, scouts were in the lobby of the hotel and at practice on Friday, where the Philadelphia 76ers were gracious enough to let the Flyers work out and get their own chance to check out Obi. It was a largely unstructured practice, with the team getting some shots up and enjoying the professional facility. The mood was light coming off a win, and the next day would be about starting the game prep for Saint Joseph's. One player, however, was going all out. Jordy Tshimanga was working on post moves with a coach at the far end of one court. By the time practice was over, he was drenched in sweat. "That comes from my family," he told me. "It's part of me. It was important for me that day to try to get better."

The team went to see a movie that night, while Keith and I went off in search of an authentic Philly cheese steak (hold the food poisoning, please). No matter what I write here, one of you readers will disagree with our choice, and that if we wanted the REAL Philly cheesesteak we should have gone to "fill in the blank." We opted for a very touristy but tasty visit to Geno's on South 9th Street. We then met some former neighbors of Keith's from when his family was still living in Kettering who were using the Flyers' trip to Philadelphia to see family on the East Coast and catch two games in one trip. With the win over La-Salle out of the way, they were now optimistic that a Philly sweep was possible.

Saint Joseph's had opened the season with wins over Bradley and UConn in two of their first three games but had just one more win before A-10 play started, losing their league opener at Richmond. This was a game on paper that the Flyers should easily win, but that was not the mind-set of the team that I saw practicing the next day at Temple's gym. As Dayton was defending against the scout team running the Hawks' offense, Ryan Mikesell and Trey Landers had both subbed out. They were watching when someone missed an assignment. Trey, who had been a vocal leader on the team now for three years, stopped the practice to point out what was wrong and correct the mistake. The next rep a different mistake was made, which Ryan corrected and then told the group on the floor, "Run it again." I looked over at Anthony Grant, who seemed pleased to have his senior leaders directing practice and taking ownership in the program. Mikesell told me there was trust between the players and coaches, "I give the coaching staff credit for their ability to simplify it and allow us to focus on just a few things. We had a really good basketball IQ. Plus, they constantly asked us for our advice and opinion on how to approach certain situations."

After completing his Hall of Fame playing career at UD, Keith Waleskowski then played professionally for nine years in Spain, Italy, and Germany. While I called upon his expertise as a player during the broadcasts, that Saturday night before the Saint Joseph's game I called upon his experience living in Italy. His former neighbors had recommended an Italian restaurant and—outside of the Peroni I ordered when we got there—I deferred to him on all other menu choices. It ended up being the dining highlight of the season. I can't recall the specific names of the dishes, but everything was delicious and, he assured me, very authentic. A win over La Salle, a Philly cheesesteak, and a gourmet meal. All that was needed now was a win at Saint Joseph's.

As I mentioned, Saint Joseph's was not a very good team coming into that Sunday afternoon game. Injuries had decimated the Hawks the previous year, and in a surprise move, the new athletic director had fired legendary coach Phil Martelli and replaced him with Billy Lange, most recently an assistant with the 76ers. Many players had transferred, and some recruits, namely Jameer Nelson Jr.—the son of the Hawks star of the 2003 team that was number one in the nation—had de-committed. Lange had his work cut out for him, and while the team had struggled to win games, they did have Ryan Daly, who was leading the league in scoring at the time, while also leading Saint Joseph's in rebounding and assists. A transfer from Delaware who had sat out the previous season, at 6'5" and 225 pounds, Daly was barrel-chested and looked like a guy you might see in a pickup game at a YMCA. He was going to be a load to handle, but did the Hawks have anyone who could handle Obi Toppin?

The Saint Joe's game plan revealed itself early. To

begin the game, they started 6'3" former walk-on Toli-
ver Freeman to guard Obi. All he did was push, shove,
and grab. If Obi caught the ball, two other Hawks
defenders would collapse on him. The Flyers took the
bait and took some less-than-ideal 3's early in the shot
clock, and the game was tied at the half at 33. Still
frustrated, Obi picked up his third foul at the 14:40
mark in the second half. Ibi Watson subbed in for him
and subsequently hit a big 3 and, over a 5-minute period, scored 13 straight points for the Flyers who hung
on for a gutsy, if not pretty, 80–67 win. The sixteen
NBA scouts in attendance got to see a mere mortal
performance by Obi with 15 points and 5 rebounds,
as he was limited to 21 minutes by foul trouble.

A scout with the Sacramento Kings had been
questioning me about Obi before the game, and Dave
Bollwinkel, who had been on Jim O'Brien's staff at
UD and was now scouting for the Chicago Bulls,
wanted to know how Obi was dealing with the media.
I told him he was a joy to be around, cooperative and
well-spoken in talking to the press, but with a boyish
charm. He would usually spend the time after his interviews trying to make his teammates crack up on
camera. The scouts may not have seen a high-flying
Toppin dunk-a-thon that day, but they witnessed a
huge stride in his development as a player. Obi had
been a good passer and a good teammate prior to that
game. After his first experience with a defense that was
totally focused on stopping him, he became a better
passer, and thus, an even better teammate. "He was
willing to accept that someone else is open and took
what the defense gave him," said GA Sean Damaska,
who had spent so much time working with Obi the
previous season. Associate Head Coach Anthony Solomon saw the same thing and the dividends it would
pay down the road. "Obi became a great passer," he

observed. "In the Saint Joseph's game, they tried to get physical with him, double- and even triple-team him. He ended up in foul trouble and sat quite a bit of the second half. After that he learned to look for the open man when he was doubled, and guys responded by knocking down shots. But as the season went on, those same teammates, when they saw he was not double-teamed, would say, "Take him, Obi.""

In his post-game radio show, Coach Grant again emphasized that it was just two games into the conference season, and the team was still a work in progress, but he acknowledged the Flyers had cleared a huge psychological, if not physical, hurdle. "We had a lot of happy Flyer fans who were able to leave this arena tonight who hadn't seen the Dayton Flyers win here in a long time," he said. "The guys even commented in the locker room, instead of coming off the floor and hearing fans say: 'congratulations' or 'great game' they heard 'thank you—thank you.' It's a blessing for us to be a part of this program and bringing joy in the new year."

NBA scouts were not the only people swarming around Obi Toppin and the Flyers. After the game, almost everyone was on the team bus waiting for Coach Grant to finish up some media interviews. A woman stepped onto the bus and asked, "Is Obi on? There are some kids who want to meet him." Without hesitation, Obi put down his post-game food and walked off the bus, where he signed autographs and posed for pictures with a growing group of people. Ultimately, Brett Comer had to get off and tell Obi to get back on the bus. In addition to his role as the Director of Player Development, Comer spent a lot of time as a mentor/bodyguard/handler for Obi. "We built a relationship first working out in the off-season," said Comer. "He would lock in and pay attention when I told him to and never resisted. He got a lot of attention, but after that first game in Maui it blew up."

I think the charter plane could have flown back to Dayton fueled simply by the sense of relief that swept through the entire travel party. Georgia/Virginia Tech/Kansas in three days had not seemed as daunting as the two Philadelphia schools to start the A-10 season. But anyone who had concerns that the massive emotional exhale would lead to complacency had those concerns addressed in the next game.

With a week to prepare while also getting to take a few days off, the Flyers hosted UMass five days after the Saint Joseph's game. The Minutemen came in 7–8 overall and had split their first two league games. The Flyer Faithful barely had time to sit down after the national anthem before Dayton had a 9–0 lead, which turned into a 26-point lead at halftime and an 88–60 final victory. Obi Toppin led a balanced scoring attack with 16 points but also added a career-high 5 steals. Ryan Mikesell also reached a new career high with 14 rebounds. All of those numbers were nearly overshadowed by one of the scariest moments of the season. With just over 15 minutes left to play in the game, Ryan Mikesell snared one of his career high rebounds on a missed 3-pointer by UMass's Tre Mitchell. Obi Toppin turned to sprint up court on offense, stepped on Mitchell's foot, and rolled his ankle. The sellout crowd was silent for the first, last, and only time in the game. Obi hobbled off the floor and then returned to the bench later in the game, wearing a protective boot.

After the game Coach Grant praised Ryan Mikesell's versatility in his radio interview. "For a guy his size at six-foot-seven, when he rebounds, having the skills to handle the ball to finish for himself, and make plays for his teammates, that's a good weapon for us to have as we move forward," he said, before addressing the injury to Obi. "Obviously, it's too early to tell. He said as he was going back, backpedaling, he stepped on someone's foot. Hopefully, the next twenty-four hours will tell us more, but we'll see what happens from there." I then asked him, "Every time you take the court you have a chance to get better, stay the same, or get worse. What happened today?" "We got better," was his quick reply. "I think we got better as a team. I think with every game our guys are understanding more and more that when we are really locked defensively like we were today, we have a chance to be a really good team, and it shows."

In contrast to the nearly week-long break before that UMass game, the Flyers faced a quick turnaround, hosting VCU on Tuesday. Not only dealing with a quick turnaround but also the uncertainty of Obi Toppin's health, Dayton was preparing to face the defending champs and the preseason favorites in the A-10. The Rams came into the game stinging from a home loss to Rhode Island, so a win by the Flyers would give them a two-game lead in the early A-10 race.

Another sellout crowd watched Obi warm up, showing no signs that his injured ankle was bothering him. The game lived up to its hype early. VCU jumped out to an early 4–0 lead, Dayton came back and regained the lead, and VCU again pulled away to lead by 5 with just over 5 minutes to play in the half. Obi then made a play that showed his ankle was bothering him, but he could adapt. Here's what it sounded like on radio: "Curry to Santos-Silva, knocked away and stolen by Obi, show time, tomahawk with the left hand, and Dayton trails by one; 31–30 with 2:45 to go!" Obi had dunked with his left hand, because he had jumped off his right foot, favoring the injured left ankle. He had not planned on it, he told me later. He just improvised on the spot. The Flyers then took the lead to go up 38–33 at the half. VCU then wiped out that lead with a 6–0 run to begin the second half. The Flyers then regained the lead on a Trey Landers 3-pointer, only to have De'Riante Jenkins dunk to tie the game at 41.

What then followed became a signature for this Dayton team. In Grant's first year, and even in the second, the Flyers had been plagued by either offensive droughts or defensive lapses that allowed opponents to go on runs, or sometimes both! With 17:35 left in the game, the Flyers exploded. Obi dunked off a feed from Mikesell. Landers finished a fast break with a layup off a pass from Crutcher, who then assisted on another Obi dunk. Obi then blocked a shot to start another fast break, finished by a Landers 3 in transition. Rodney Chatman hit a floater in the lane. Obi was the assist man on a Landers dunk. Crutcher scored off of a Rams turnover and then assisted on yet another dunk by Obi. Obi then stepped out and drained a 3. Ibi Watson scored inside. When VCU's Vince Williams hit a free throw with just under 11 minutes to go, that ended a 22–0 Flyers run. The Rams got as close as 10 before Obi Toppin added the exclamation mark to the win: "Crutcher driving, lobbing, Obi with the catch and the flush." After two losses to VCU in the closing seconds the previous season, the Flyers had rolled over the Rams and staked their own claim as the best team in the A-10. Marcus Evans, one of the preseason favorites to be Player of the Year in the league, was held to 13 points on 5-for-12 shooting from the field. Obi Toppin played 34 minutes on a sore ankle and scored 23 points, pulled down 9 rebounds, had 3 assists, a block, and steal. His roommate, the Peanut Butter half of Peanut Butter and Jam, had 20 points and 5 assists.

Dayton had exorcised some demons: a pair of wins in Philadelphia, a rout of UMass, and the complete second-half dominance of the defending A-10 champs. The Flyers were sitting at 15–2 overall, 4–0 in the Atlantic Ten, heading into their first true road test of the season.

Bucky Bockhorn and Larry

12

A MISSING LEGEND

WHILE THE POSTSEASON AND A POSSIBLE National Championship was glaringly absent from the 2019–2020 season, there was another noticeable absence.

For the first time in over forty-five years, Arlen "Bucky" Bockhorn was not behind the microphone for a single game. The self-proclaimed Legend earned that title first as a player and a broadcaster and remains one of the most beloved figures in Flyer basketball history.

"I'm from Resume Speed," Bucky will often say, self-deprecatingly.

This may be one time when he does not exaggerate. Campbell Hill was a small town in Illinois when Bucky was growing up, and little, if anything has changed. Since 1996 there has not been a single new home constructed in the town. The population hovers around 351. Today, most of the residents still claim a

German heritage, much as it was when the Bockhorn family was working their farm back in the Depression.

Bucky was born July 8, 1933, and his memories of the Depression are not about hardship within his household, but without. "I can remember vagrants showing up at the door to ask Mom for food," he remembered. "We'd hide behind her skirts, scared of these skinny, hard-looking men. Mom always had something for them, so I guess we were doing okay. Another big event was when the ragman came around. Mom could buy rags, and pots and pans and stuff. Us kids just liked to see what all he had."

There were a few rare trips to Carbondale to go to the movies, but for the most part recreation was the farm. Most people raised on farms that I talk to describe the same kind of mix of business and pleasure that Bucky talks about in his youth. There were trees to climb, ponies to ride, creeks to swim in, but also cows to milk, chickens to feed, and wood to cut.

"We would always come across stray dogs and bring them home. My dad would say, 'They can stay as long as they ain't egg-suckers.' And sure enough, if he caught one in the henhouse, he'd take it out in the barn and shoot it," Bucky recalled. "We'd get a little upset, but we understood early on, those eggs meant a lot more to the family than any dog."

The "city-life" aspect of growing up in Campbell Hill was Ray and Francis's Bar. Bucky's dad would stop by on his way home from the coal mine to drink beer and shots and play the slot machines. He was a hard worker and a hard drinker. Bucky speaks of him respectfully, but not fondly. His mother was the leader of the family. She was a large woman, aged prematurely by seven kids and the daily toil of farm life. But she was a strong woman with enough love to go around for her girls and boys.

In an earlier book written about the NBA, Bucky's mother was quoted as saying: "Arlen was such a happy child, riding his pony through the valley and yodeling all the way." Do you think he took some ribbing about that from teammates and opponents?

In 1949 Trico High School in Campbell Hill had 14 teachers and 250 students. One of them was Arlen "Bucky" Bockhorn. "We had a good team but went through a slump where we would come out at the start of the games playing terrible. So, Coach [Lynne Irvine Jr.] would have us scrimmage full-go for fifteen minutes before the game started. It worked, and we started playing better."

Bucky had a good enough career at Trico to be inducted into that school's Hall of Fame and have his number retired. He's also in the Illinois State High School Hall of Fame, the University of Dayton Athletic Hall of Fame, the Cincinnati Basketball Hall of Fame, on the UD Silver Anniversary Team, and on the UD All-Century Team. One would think someone who has received that kind of recognition who calls himself the Legend would bask in such attention. It could not be farther from the truth.

For someone who has hit clutch shots in front of thousands of fans and who has talked on radio for nearly forty years, Bucky is painfully shy about speaking in public. While he appreciates every one of the honors he has received, each time it brings with it the fear of having to make an acceptance speech.

Such was the case when he was to have his number retired at Trico High School in 1995. His school friend Nick Dolce contacted me in regard to openings on the Flyers basketball schedule that season that would allow Bucky to make the trip to Campbell Hill without missing a broadcast. A date was picked in late December and Bucky began sweating—and practicing. He had me help him with the talk on the plane flying out to Hawaii where the Flyers were playing in the Rainbow Classic over the Thanksgiving holiday. After a disappointing loss to the host University of Hawaii in the first game, I got to hear Bucky practice the speech several more times before Dayton pulled off an upset of LSU in the second night. We flew back to the mainland feeling optimistic about the season ahead, despite Bucky's dread of his return home in the next month.

Prior to the next six games Bucky would practice the speech by walking out to the center circle of the court and speaking toward me at press row. I coached him up, and by the time the day for the ceremonies in Campbell Hill arrived, he was ready, but Mother Nature was not. The game at Trico High School was snowed out, and so Bucky's special night was postponed until mid-February . . . when it snowed again! Finally, in the spring, without benefit of a high school game to hold the ceremonies, Bucky's number 46 jersey became the first and only jersey retired in Trico High School history. I didn't make the trip to Southern Illinois, because—what the heck—I had heard the acceptance speech nearly one hundred times already!

His Hall of Fame high school career attracted the attention of one of Dayton Coach Tom Blackburn's bird-dog scouts, Joe Fisher. Fisher drove to Campbell Hill along with Flyer players Jack Sallee and Jim Paxson, picked up Bucky the summer after he graduated from Trico in 1952, packed his bags, and took him to Dayton.

After playing freshman ball at UD, Bucky was drafted during the Korean War and served two years in the army, posted in Fort Lewis, Washington. He never shipped overseas and sharpened his game by playing for the base basketball team while growing and maturing. He returned to campus in 1955 and was part of teams that won 25, 19, and 25 games, finishing as the runners-up in the NIT in both 1956 and 1958. He was a fierce competitor, a tenacious defender, and a rugged rebounder. His was the type of blue-collar effort that won over fans in a blue-collar town.

He was drafted by the Cincinnati Royals in 1958 and enjoyed a seven-year professional career, again known mainly as a defender and the backcourt mate of Hall of Famer Oscar Robertson. "I just took the ball out of bounds for Oscar," he often says.

As usual, he is underselling himself. For his NBA career Bucky averaged 11.5 points, 4.7 rebounds, and 3.5 assists per game. And he and Robertson are one of just nine NBA teammates to both record triple-doubles in the same game. Playing the Philadelphia Warriors in 1962, Oscar had 28 points, 14 rebounds, and 16 assists, while Bucky chipped in 19 points, 10 rebounds, and 12 assists.

He played in an era in which there were just nine teams in the NBA. Roster spots were so dear, players fought for their jobs, literally.

"There was a fight almost every night," he recalls. "And even if you didn't want to fight, you would have a 'dance partner' on an opposing team: someone you could square off with and that way look like you were being a team player."

He still holds a grudge against a former Temple Owl who was playing with the Warriors.

"Guy Rodgers sucker-punched me in the mouth," he says, removing a plate with two false teeth. "And then he went and hid behind Wilt!"

Bucky's hard-nosed and unselfish play earned the respect and support of his teammates. The Cincinnati Royals (now the Sacramento Kings) were playing at the St. Louis Hawks (now the Atlanta Hawks). That was relatively close to Bucky's hometown in southern Illinois, so his mom and dad would go to the games. His coal-mining farmer of a father thought sports was a waste of time and never watched Bucky play in high school or college. Bucky had two brothers, Terry and Harold, who joined him at UD. Their dad stopped by Ray and Francis's Bar in Campbell Hill on the way home from the mine one day. The NIT was on the television above the bar. One of the patrons said:

"Look, Elvie, your boys are on TV in New York City."

"Well, I'll be damned," was his reply.

Now that his son had turned playing basketball into a solid career, though not as lucrative as today's game, the Bockhorn patriarch would go to the games in St. Louis. Bucky said he never played well in those games, perhaps trying too hard to impress his dad.

One game some fans behind one basket were razzing him pretty hard: "Arlen, what the hell kind of name is Arlen?" On and on they went with that refrain. Bucky's ears were getting red with anger when teammate Wayne Embry pulled him aside. "I'll take care of those guys," Embry said. "The next time you get a defensive rebound, just turn and throw a long outlet pass."

Bucky got a rebound and threw the ball to the far end of the court, with Embry lumbering in pursuit, with no real possibility of catching up to it. That was not his intent, anyway. As he reached the end of the court, he launched his 6'8" 240-pound body into the seats behind the basket where Bucky's tormentors were sitting. Popcorn and beer went flying, and they never called him Arlen for the rest of the game.

When his playing career was cut short by a knee injury in the 1964–1965 season, he took a job as a salesman with a chemical company in Cincinnati. Shortly thereafter, Dayton Athletic Director Tom Frericks suggested he get into broadcasting and arranged a meeting with the Commissioner of the Mid-American Conference. Bucky worked as a TV analyst for the MAC game of the week. He was part of a rotation of former Flyers who worked as analysts for games on WHIO-TV. In 1972, he joined another former Flyer, Chris Harris, as the radio broadcast team, first on WONE for three years, and then at WHIO.

In 1982 Harris moved to Seattle, working in the insurance business. I had been at WHIO for just over a year, working as the producer of Lou Emm's morning show, and as the Radio Sports Director. I immediately threw my hat in the ring, with the support of then WHIO General Manager Ron Kempff. My candidacy was met with underwhelming enthusiasm by Mr. Frericks. He did not want to entrust the Flyer broadcast to a twenty-six-year-old kid whose only previous experience had been calling high school games in places like Montpelier, Stryker, Archbold, and Hicksville. A search for a more viable candidate even included an offer to Marty Brennaman, who declined due to conflicts with his Reds spring training schedule. Through it all, Bucky had stood in my corner, even though at the time we barely knew each other. Tom Frericks had us call some Flyer intra-squad scrimmages on tape and after reviewing a few tapes gave his blessing. To his credit, from that moment on until his dying day, he was unwavering in his support of me and my work.

As I detailed in the book that I wrote in 2014, *True Team: The Dayton Flyers' Run to the Elite Eight*, Bucky took me under his wing those early years of my career, and it is my turn to look out for him. From 1982 through the 1998–1999 season, he and I worked together. Occasionally, I would miss a basketball broadcast due to a conflict with Flyer football. The only UD basketball game I worked with someone other than Bucky was the 1986 NIT. Dayton played at McNeese State and the game was broadcast on both WHIO-TV and WHIO Radio. However, Channel 7's Mick Hubert was scheduled to work NCAA tournament games for CBS, so UD and Channel 7 opted to have Bucky move over to TV to work alongside Mike Hartsock, while the late Gene Schill, who was then an Associate Athletic Director at Dayton, joined me on the radio.

To start the 2014–2015 season, Bucky decided he wanted to spend some time in Orlando, watching his grandson, also named Arlen in his honor, play high school basketball. He had earned the right to step away from the mic for a few games. He was hesitant at first, because in the era in which he grew up, if you didn't show up for work, someone would have your job the next day. I assured him that he could do whatever he wanted.

He worked the season opener vs. Alabama A&M and then headed to Florida. Former Flyer Brooks Hall went with me to Puerto Rico. He, Keith Waleskowski, and Josh Postorino rotated through the analyst's role for the next few weeks, with Bucky coming back to work with me for the last non-conference game vs. Ole Miss.

He missed some road games the rest of that season, and I even missed the UMass and Fordham games due to back surgery. Josh Postorino worked the A-10 tournament, and then Bucky and I rejoined for the NCAA Tournament, a First Four win over Boise State before a raucous crowd at the UD Arena, a win over Providence before another very partisan fan base in Columbus, and then the shorthanded Flyers running out of gas with a loss to Oklahoma.

The next two seasons, Bucky worked very few road games but was there for NCAA tournament losses against Syracuse in St. Louis in 2016 and vs. Wichita State in Indianapolis in 2017.

When Archie Miller left for Indiana, Bucky called me. "I'm done. I just don't have the energy to go through a coaching change."

I called him the following week when I first learned that Anthony Grant got the job. "I'm back!" he said.

That 2017–2018 season he worked all of the home games and just a handful of road games. On the afternoon of a game at George Mason, he called me from his hotel room. He had broken out in a rash, similar to the allergic reaction he had in Memphis in 2014 after eating something that had been cross-contaminated by shellfish. I gave him a shot with the EpiPen he had carried ever since, but it did little to help. Dayton Trainer Mike Mulcahey advised him to see the George Mason doctor once we arrived at their arena. Against doctor's orders he worked the game, struggling with a swollen tongue. Once we got back to Dayton, his primary care physician determined it was a reaction to his blood pressure medication, but he was told not to travel the rest of the season. That turned out to be the final road game for Bucky, as he did only home games in 2018–2019.

Like most Flyer fans, he was eagerly anticipating the 2019–2020 season and spent the summer watching the players working out. He had seen the potential of Jordy Tshimanga, Rodney Chatman, Ibi Watson, and Chase Johnson while they were sitting out their transfer season, but he was also seeing how they blended with the returning players like Obi Toppin, Trey Landers, Jalen Crutcher, and Ryan Mikesell.

However, as the season approached, Bucky was struggling with his mobility and was able to attend fewer and fewer practices. By October he was nearly chair-bound or bedridden by pain in his hip. He waved off working the exhibition game vs. Cedarville and again for the season opener vs. Indiana State. As each day passed, his optimism would be squelched by a physical setback. He missed the Charleston Southern and Omaha games.

All the while he was being treated for a ruptured bursa sac in his hip. He was getting injections but no relief. He was on a waiting list to get an MRI so as to have surgery. The pain kept getting worse.

Before I left with the team for Maui, I called his son Dan and asked if I could get involved in his father's treatment. He gave me the green light and I contacted Mulcahey, who in turn was able to get Bucky an appointment with Dr. Townsend Smith, who specializes in pain treatment. He has given me more injections in my back through the years than I can count.

After seeing Dr. Smith and getting an injection, Bucky went through some physical therapy. The pain had eased but had not disappeared. The MRI revealed a herniated disc in his lower back. On December 21, 2019, while the Flyers were getting ready to play Colorado in Chicago, Dr. James Lehner operated on his back. I spoke to Bucky's wife, Peggy, right after the procedure and all went well. However, the next day he fell down trying to go to the bathroom. That extended his hospital stay until Christmas Day, when he then got an ambulance ride to Bethany Lutheran Village for rehab.

Bucky stayed in rehab until January 4, while the Flyers were opening up A-10 play with games at La Salle and Saint Joseph's in Philadelphia. The team planned on coming to his home for a visit, but he waved us all off.

Throughout this time, I would pop over to his

house and visit, watching football games on TV and having a few cold beers. He was very engaged with the Flyer season and had a stack of box scores and current stats next to his recliner. We would talk basketball, and he was optimistic that once he regained strength in his legs, he could return to the Arena.

He received a few weeks of in-home therapy, and I came to the last session to see what was being done. I took notes on all of the exercises as well as his reaction to doing them.

One of the many hats I wear is that of a personal trainer. After one of my back surgeries, a cervical fusion in 2004, I began working with a trainer, Charles Baerman, to get my strength back. As I continued to get even stronger than I had been pre-surgery, Charles told me that I had a good understanding of exercise science plus an ability to communicate. I studied and took the test, and then in 2008 started working at Personal Fit in Moraine. Many of my clients since that time have been older, so I felt that I could be able to help my friend and broadcast partner.

The first thing I did was eliminate two exercises that his therapist had him doing that caused him pain and that he hated doing! There were plenty of ways to get his legs stronger and improve his core strength and balance without making him hurt or dread working out.

We seemed to make progress through the weeks. I would bring in some broasted chicken and potato salad from Dot's Supermarket in Bellbrook. We would go through the exercises together and I would give him some new ones to do on the days I was not there. All the while the season continued with Keith or Brooks usually sitting next to me for the broadcast. Josh Postorino had moved to Phoenix but was still working for UD in Development. He worked the game vs. Saint Mary's with me in Phoenix for obvious reasons—and also worked the Colorado game in Chicago, the two games in Richmond against the Spiders, and the VCU Rams. He was also with me in Brooklyn when the season came to an abrupt end.

I made out a schedule for the rest of the season, with the understanding that whenever Bucky wanted to work, that game was his. The guys were more than understanding. Bucky means as much to them as former players as he does to the fans.

Even though he was getting stronger, Bucky had a new reason for not wanting to come back to the broadcasts. He was afraid of jinxing the team, which was in the midst of what would be a 20-game winning streak!

"When I played pro ball, I put on my socks the same way and ate the same thing for pre-game meals. I was very superstitious then, and I still am now."

Finally, he broke down and went to a practice the week of the Davidson game. Obviously, the team was thrilled to see him, and he decided that he would work the regular season finale vs. George Washington. His concern, though, was that he didn't want his presence to take any attention away from the seniors.

"Are you kidding me," I said. "You BEING there would MAKE their Senior Night!"

The plan was in place. I would pick him up, drive to the Arena. There was a parking space by the back door where I could drop him off. We could either take the new elevator down to the floor level, or he could be driven down on the golf cart.

I called him from Rhode Island to check on him, and he told me that he had fallen in the shower. Luckily, my friend Gary Pascoe had installed some extra grab bars in the shower, and he was able to pull himself off the floor. However, the progress made in working out the past weeks went down that shower drain. He told me he would not work on Saturday.

I asked him to reconsider on Thursday, after we got back from Rhode Island, and again on Friday. I even called him Saturday morning during the *Game Day* broadcast and made one last plea. "I really think if you don't come out tonight, you'll regret it," I said. "No. I'm just too weak," he replied. "But I am not done. I will be back next season!"

Keith Waleskowski worked alongside me that night, as the Flyers punctuated their A-10 Championship season with a demolition of George Washington in the second half, and Keith did a good job, as always. He, Brooks, and Josh all bring something unique to the table of value to the listeners.

But they are not Bucky.

There is only one Legend.

UD Arena Security guard Mike Galbraith

13

CLUTCHER

THE DAYTON FLYERS HAD YET TO PLAY before a hostile crowd. The Flyer Faithful had outnumbered all other schools at the Maui Invitational, the Jerry Colangelo Classic in Phoenix, and the Chicago Legends. It was a smaller Dayton crowd at La Salle, but again, more than there were fans of the Explorers. Even Saint Joseph's, where the Hawks traditionally pack the place with their fans, saw their own struggles result in Dayton fans able to get tickets in abundance. It sounded like a home game in the second half with chants of "We are—UD!"

Dayton knew it would be a different scenario in St. Louis, where the Chaifetz Arena seats 10,600, the Billikens were sitting just a game back in the A-10 at 3–1, and their fans consider the Flyers to be their league rivals. The potentially hostile environment was part of the reason for an addition to the traveling party and that trip, and for every road game thereafter.

Mike Galbraith retired from the Dayton Police Department after thirty years in 2016. He began working security at the UD Arena in 1991 and for the past fifteen years had been stationed behind the home bench. His duties included getting the team off and on the floor safely and accompanying Coach Grant to press row for his post-game radio show and then to the media interview room afterwards. He was a natural choice for an additional assignment. "After the trip to Philly I was asked to travel with the team. They were trying to deal with autograph seekers and people trying to get to Obi," he told me. "I heard agents were pressuring Obi's mom." I had known Mike since he had started working security at the Arena, and he would often sit with me on the plane. I was amazed at how he would insulate the team from outsiders without overtly inserting himself in the situations. Occasionally, he would have to be more direct, especially with autograph seekers who began hanging out in front of hotels and arenas, awaiting the Flyers' arrival. "I had to be aware of our surroundings and try to avoid crowds," he said. "I never got confrontational with people who try to get pushy when asking for autographs. Some of them called me names, but nothing I didn't hear in thirty years on the police force."

While Mike stayed with the team in the hotel, Brooks Hall, who was working the game with me, joined me, SID Doug Hauschild, AD Neil Sullivan, and Associate Athletic Director Rob Poteat at Charlie Gitto's in downtown St. Louis. Bob DeMarco played football at UD before embarking on a fourteen-year NFL career, the first eight of which were spent in St. Louis, where he remains a local legend. After his playing career he was a salesman for the same chemical company for which Bucky Bockhorn worked, and when the Flyers played in St. Louis, Bucky and I would have dinner with him at Charlie Gitto's. It was an Italian restaurant where the excellent food was matched, if not surpassed, by the pictures of athletes, entertainers, and other types of celebrities that adorned the wall. Bob introduced us to Charlie himself, and Charlie's son-in-law was from Dayton. Whenever the Flyers were in town, they were expecting us. There is now a picture of Charlie, Bob DeMarco, Bucky, and me on the wall, which they had us sign. I guess if you eat at a restaurant only once a year but you do it for over thirty years, they remember you. We've been there on Friday nights when the place was packed with Mardi Gras revelers and Monday evenings when the downtown streets and most of their tables were empty. One time we even had some police officers give us a ride back to our hotel on their golf carts. Dinner this night was magnificent, as usual. I had eggplant parmigiana, which is one of my go-to dishes on the menu. Everyone else enjoyed their meal and the chance to talk with Charlie and his grandson, who saw to it we received special treatment. Sadly, Charlie passed away in July of 2020 from a heart attack.

People often ask me who Dayton's rival is. Since the departure of Xavier from the A-10 and their reticence to play a non-conference game, I am quick to say Saint Louis. There is a history of playing the Billikens that predates any conference affiliation, and UD and SLU have been in the same league in the MCC, the Great Midwest, and now the A-10. Even though both programs have had a few dry years, the games are usually very competitive and meaningful in terms of league race and national profile. That was the case this time around. Dayton entered with a 4–0 mark in the A-10, while Saint Louis was 3–1. Quite simply, if the Flyers won, they would open some more daylight. If the Billikens won, they would share first place. Underscoring the rivalry nature of the game, Saint Louis was holding a "white-out" at Chaifetz Arena, with white T-shirts draped across every seat, except for those behind the UD bench that were allocated to Flyer fans.

Rebounding had been the Flyers' Achilles' heel the previous two seasons vs. SLU, and again Hasahn French and Jordan Goodwin came in among the leaders in the A-10 in offensive rebounding. Gibson Jimerson, who had impressed me with his 3-point shooting when I saw the Billikens play in Phoenix, was out with a season-ending injury. With no real perimeter threat, their best offensive play was a missed shot. As expected, the first half was a physical battle, and as feared Saint Louis dominated on the glass, outrebounding the Flyers 27–17 to take a 33–25 lead, holding Dayton to its lowest first-half total of the season. The sellout crowd was smelling an upset, which made Mike Galbraith's job as security guard even more difficult. "Getting players on and off the court through the student body was a challenge," he told me.

The half ended with Obi Toppin missing a follow-up dunk off a Crutcher miss with one second to play. It's a shot I never saw him miss before or after. Coach Grant spent some time walking off the floor with him (with the protection afforded by Galbraith!). "I just tried to give him some perspective on what he needed to do," said Grant afterwards. "And what the situation was. That we had another 20 minutes in a three-possession game that he was going to be a big part of."

The Flyers cut it to 4 before Saint Louis went on a run to lead 53–40 with 8:45 to play. I could almost feel radios and TVs switching off as fans back in Dayton looked for better ways to spend their Friday evening than witnessing an inevitable defeat. Helping fuel that pessimism, Dayton was 2-for-16 from three-point range at that point in the game.

Then something happened. Obi scored after rebounding a miss by Ibi Watson to cut the lead to 11. After Saint Louis responded with a bucket by freshman point guard Yuri Collins, Watson answered with a short jumper. Ibi then hit a 3. Crutcher hit a 3. Trey Landers made a pair of free throws. Watson and Obi hit back-to-back 3's, and when Landers drained a 3-pointer with 3:10 to play, Dayton had its first lead since the first half. French tied the game on a rare-made free throw (he was 4-for-10 in the game). Obi nailed a 3 at the top of the key to regain the lead for the Flyers. After making just two of their first 16 3-point attempts, four players had combined to make six in a row. In the post-game radio show I said to Coach Grant, "What does it say about the character of this team that on a night where a lot of guys might say, 'We're 2 of 16, we just don't have it,' but they kept fighting?" Coach replied,

> That's not this team. We got a time-out and we talked about "here's what we need to do down the stretch." No matter what. No matter what the outcome is. They ran the huddle in terms of what we're doing. We've been here before. We've been through this. We're going to find a way. We're going to win this game.

Obi added another jumper to take the lead out to 5 with just under 2 minutes to go. Saint Louis would not go away. Two free throws and a jumper by Javonte Perkins cut the Dayton lead to 1. Trey Landers took it back out to 3 with a layup, but then Rodney Chatman missed the front end of a one-and-one. Jordan Goodwin hit two free throws and Chatman missed another front end. Trey Landers then pulled down a huge defensive rebound off a miss by Goodwin and stepped to the line shooting two, with Dayton leading 68–67 with 5 seconds to play. He missed the first and made the second, Goodwin rushed the ball up court, and made a tough layup with one second to go. "I should have called a time-out there. That's on me," said Grant in the post-game show. "But Goodwin comes down and makes a helluva play."

Dayton heads to overtime for the third time in the season, having suffered its only two losses, to Kansas and Colorado, in OT. Saint Louis took a 2-point lead to begin overtime, as Hasahn French was wide right on a pair of free throws, but was able to also make two. Ibi Watson tied the game for Dayton at 71. Yuri Collins regained the lead for SLU, making one of two from the line. Jalen Crutcher hit a pair to put Dayton up 73–72. Crutcher added two more free throws and the Flyers led 75–74 with 17 seconds to play. After a time-out, Saint Louis put the ball in the hands of freshman Collins, who attacked the rim and was fouled. "I called him over and the freshman [Yuri Collins] was on the line, and he wasn't necessarily a great free throw shooter," said Grant. "So, I told him here's what we're going to do, anticipating a miss. I gave him the action we wanted to run. He went back and let the team know."

What followed still gives me chills. Here's what Brooks Hall and I said on radio:

Me: "Three seconds. Crutcher. Three. Good if it goes. It does! It does! It does! With one-tenth of a second to play!"

Brooks: "Jalen CLUTCHER!"

Me: "CLUTCHER comes through. In bounds.

No good. No good! The Dayton Flyers have won on a 3-pointer by Jalen Crutcher in overtime!"

Saint Louis was in shock as they came off the floor. Their student body was stunned, shaken so badly they watched in silence as the Flyers celebrated in front of their bench along with a knot of fans, many of them Crutcher's relatives who had made the trip from Memphis. David Gasper was among the group of Dayton fans and was surprised to see Crutcher's mom joining the festivities late. "Where you been?" he told me he had asked her. She said she had been too nervous in the overtime and had been walking along the concourse level.

Jalen finished with 21 points and was a perfect 4-for-4 from the line in overtime. His game-winning 3 overshadowed a bone-jarring screen set by his roommate and best friend Obi Toppin that freed him up with just enough space to get a clean look at the rim. What was perhaps most impressive, however, was that with just six seconds to work, he was never rushed and out of control. "That's something you work on in practice," said Grant. "We call them special situations in terms of the clock and where you are on the floor. But I thought he did a great job with his poise and calmness to come down and make that play."

A. J. Schraffenberger had joined the staff as a content creator for the team's social media. Initially, players were suspicious of a guy following their every move with a camera. "As they got to know me, they became more comfortable," he told me after the season. "Knowing the person behind the camera allowed them to show their true personality." That game became his personal highlight of the season, both from the video memories it produced, and also from the impact on the team's success. "Watching Jalen hit that shot against Saint Louis was amazing, given the whole atmosphere that night with their sellout crowd," he recalled. "Lots of people saw the video of the locker room celebration, how the guys all dumped water on Jalen and Obi when they came in after doing post-game TV stuff. Jordy picked up a giant cooler of water to dump on Obi. It was just pure joy."

Brooks Hall worked that game with me on radio, and he was no stranger to last-second dramatics. I can still picture him under a dog pile on the Arena floor following his game winner against Villanova in 2002. However, in reflecting on that moment in St. Louis, he was hard pressed to find one that eclipsed "Clutcher's" shot. "Everybody was waiting for them to lose, and a loss at that point probably would have rocked their seeding and ranking potential," he said. "Given all of that, and the environment, Saint Louis is a tough place to play, that might have been the biggest shot I have seen, including mine to beat Villanova."

It was a game that might have been a defining moment for the season. Perhaps at the time, Coach Grant sensed that in his post-game comments to me. "Our guys showed unbelievable heart. Unbelievable character. Unbelievable fight. I told them after the game, that these are the types of games that championship-caliber teams win."

It was a clutch performance by a clutch team with a clutch player who did not avoid the moment when the game was on the line. And Jalen CLUTCHER was just warming up.

UD managers in Maui: Alex Reilly, Henry Stark, Alex Roberts, and Matt Weckesser

14

CHALLENGES MET

ONE WEEK BEFORE JALEN CRUTCHER HIT his game-winning shot at Saint Louis, Chase Johnson announced on Instagram that he would not be returning to school for the second semester, focusing instead on the medical issues arising from post-concussive syndrome. While he was no longer around the team, the Flyers did add another player to the roster. Zimi Nwokeji, a 6'7" forward from Florida, had backed out of his verbal commitment to Florida State—and after reopening his recruitment, a relationship between his prep school coach and Flyers Associate Head Coach Anthony Solomon resulted in him signing with Dayton after a short recruitment. He left his prep school and enrolled at the University of Dayton for the second semester. He was with the team practicing as was redshirt Moulaye Sissoko. Both of them provided an "insurance policy" if the ranks thinned, but the plan was for both of them to redshirt and learn, preparing for the future.

After the first of the year, the Flyers rose to 15th in the AP poll, to 13th heading into the Saint Louis game, and after the win over the Billikens, cracked the top ten at No.7. The Friday win over Saint Louis gave the team a weekend to exhale before preparing to host St. Bonaventure that Wednesday. Dayton stayed unbeaten in A-10 play and ran its streak to eight in a row, blowing out the Bonnies. The Flyers jumped out to a 6–0 lead and never trailed in an 86–60 rout. Jalen Crutcher followed up his heroics in Saint Louis with 23 points and 7 assists including an alley-oop to Ryan Mikesell for a two-handed jam that brought the house down. "That was the favorite dunk of my career," recalled Mikesell. I came away impressed with the way in which Dayton had made a good St. Bonaventure team look quite ordinary and almost toothless in comparison. In addition to a sellout crowd, the game against the Bonnies marked a season high for the number of NBA scouts in attendance. Sports Information Director Doug Hauschild said there was an average of ten at every game, but that night he issued nineteen scouting credentials, including multiples for front office personnel of the Pistons, Cavs, Heat, and Bucks.

If the Flyers had surprised some of the pre-season predictors in the A-10 (except me . . . see first chapter), another team which had not garnered much attention before the season and was putting together a nice year was Richmond. Richmond was just a game behind the Flyers in the A-10 at 5–1 and with a No. 7 ranking on their back, came into a Saturday home game against the Flyers ready to make a statement.

Josh Postorino flew in from Phoenix to meet up with the travel party in Richmond. We had a Friday night meal with some boosters and then sat in on the film and scouting report session the following day. I was impressed with not just how the coaches were breaking down Richmond's offense and defense, but also the way in which the players were absorbing the information. It was an interactive process with questions and even suggestions being offered by the players. Anthony Solomon thought it was one of the strengths of this team. "We had a sound base of guys familiar with the program," he told me. "They would ask quality and respectful questions. They asked about how to do something, not why we were doing it."

The game was slated to tip-off at 6:00 p.m. We typically arrive at the venue ninety minutes prior to game time. The Richmond student body was waiting for us. The Spiders baseball team was out in force and were bare-chested and painted, standing behind the basket at the end of the court near the Dayton bench. As soon as the Flyers walked on the floor, the Spiders were in full voice, directing most of their taunts at Obi, while serenading all the players with chants of "overrated!" Instead of blocking them out, Obi engaged the hecklers in conversation and was laughing through most of the pre-game warmups. "Our fans are amazing. They bring a lot of energy and it gives us energy," Obi said. "Away fans are energy boosters, too!" While the coaching staff always sought to keep Obi focused and dialed in, Ricardo Greer saw that Toppin was the type of player who needed to play loose. "To be honest with you," Greer told me, "sometimes the game was too easy for him. It was important for him to be having fun."

Anyone who has ever played a sport at any level—from ping pong in a basement to team sports at the highest level—can agree the best way to have fun is to win. Dayton checked both boxes on that Saturday night in the capital of Virginia. Despite a brief

Richmond lead around the midway point of the first half, the Flyers wiped that out with a 9–0 run and led by 8 at the half, 40–32. In that first half Dayton was playing defense in front of the Spiders student section. In the second half, they would have a front row seat for the Flyers coming at them on offense. The Flyers went on a 12–0 run over a 5-minute period to open some daylight. It was the type of second-half run that would become a signature of this team. I credit these runs to two things. First, this team was incredibly efficient and unselfish on offense, but trading baskets does not a "run" make. It also takes stop after stop at the defensive end. I go back to how the team had digested the scouting report that morning. By the midpoint of the second half, Richmond had abandoned their offense, as Dayton had defended it so well. Ironically, it almost cost the Flyers the game. Two talented Richmond players—Jacob Gilyard and Nick Sherrod—started going one-on-one and jacking 3's. Some of them went in, and the Flyers saw their lead cut to 8. Jalen Crutcher hit a 3, part of his new season high of 23 points, and Trey Landers did what Trey Landers did all season—and really in his sophomore and junior seasons as well—and that is make big baskets when needed, putting back an offensive rebound to put Dayton up 13 with under 3 minutes to play.

The Flyers' 87–79 win was one of their more impressive victories of the year, coming on the road against a quality opponent. Obi silenced the hecklers in the second half with a breakaway windmill dunk, which Ryan Mikesell pantomimed behind him, while Zimi Nwokeji jumped nearly as high on the bench. Dayton came away from hostile environments at Saint Louis and at Richmond unscathed, on the scoreboard, and literally to the relief of security guard Mike Galbraith. "I was worried about fans coming out on the court," he later told me. "I had my eyes on some guys sitting behind the basket."

It was a great Flyer victory but somewhat marred by the officiating. I won't get into specifics, but both Anthony Grant and Richmond Coach Chris Mooney drew technical fouls. These are two of the less volatile coaches in the A-10, so them both being enraged enough to warrant getting "T'd" up speaks volumes about the job of the men in stripes that night. It underscores an issue that has existed in the Atlantic Ten for as long as I can remember, Saturday crews are notoriously not made up of some of the best-rated officials available. Whether it is for economic or prestigious reasons, the more experienced and more highly thought-of officials are working Big Ten, Big East, or ACC games instead.

Dayton was back on the road the following week to play a Wednesday night game at Duquesne, in what proved to be a pivotal game in the season. Like Anthony Grant, Duquesne coach Keith Dambrot was in his third season at the Pittsburgh school. He had completely revamped the roster over that period. After a successful fourteen-year career at Akron where he failed to win twenty games only once—in his first year—he had finished 16–16 in his first year at Duquesne, followed up by a 19–13 record, including a 10–8 mark in the A-10. Coming into this matchup with the Flyers, who were holding at No. 7 in the AP poll, Duquesne was 5–2 in the A-10. UD was 7–0. Again, it was an opportunity for both teams: for Dayton, a chance to put more space between themselves and another contender, while a Duquesne win would leave them just a game behind the Flyers.

Duquesne was playing without a true home court this season, using the UMPC Events Center on the campus of Robert Morris University for some games and PPG Paints Arena, the home of the NHL's Penguins, for others. Despite being nomads, the Dukes were undefeated at whatever venue they were calling home. This game was being played at the spacious PPG Paints Arena, and a quick scan of the crowd leading up to tip-off showed more fans for Dayton on hand than for the hometown Dukes.

Dayton took an early lead, with Jalen Crutcher joining the 1,000-point club with his first bucket. Duquesne came back to tie it up, only to have the Flyers pull away for an 8-point, 38–30 halftime lead. One of the exasperating plays of the first half was Dukes center Michael Hughes banking in a 3-pointer, as he had the previous year at the UD Arena. It was one of just two he made to that point all season. In addition to his 3 in the first half in this game, he hit two more in the second and another in the second meeting at the UD Arena in February. Against the Flyers in 2019–2020, Michael Hughes was 4-for-7 from three-point range and 1-for-11 in all other games.

I would describe an 8-point lead as a good working margin, but by no means comfortable. However, Dayton appeared to be ready to deliver the killer blow. Jalen Crutcher hit a 3 to start the second half, and after back-to-back Obi Toppin dunks, Duquesne was forced to use a quick time-out. Marcus Weathers scored a pair of baskets on strong post moves to stop the bleeding for the Dukes, but when Ibi Watson hit a short jumper in the lane, Dayton had a 57–38 lead with just over 12 minutes to go. And then for the first, and fortunately last time this season, the Flyers relaxed. Coming out of a media time-out, Dayton was flat-footed and simply watched as Tavian Dunn-Martin drained a wide-open 3. Dunn-Martin then stole the inbound pass and hit another 3. Obi Toppin missed a jumper, and even though Dunn-Martin missed a layup at the other end, Baylee Steele scored on an offensive rebound. Crutcher answered with a bucket, but then Sincere Carry hit a 3 and Dunn-Martin stole the ball from Obi feeding Michael Hughes for a dunk. Dayton's lead was cut to 8, and Anthony Grant could not afford to wait for the under-8 media time-out, calling a 30-second time-out with 8:42 to go. The game went back and forth over the next 4 minutes, and then Dayton called another time-out, leading now by just 6.

Keith Waleskowski and I were broadcasting from the scorer's table side of the floor, right next to the Dayton bench. This is not the best vantage point, as usually Coach Grant is standing right in front of us through much of the game. I have to bob and weave around him in order to get a look at what is happening on the floor. After the game at Saint Louis, I was physically exhausted, trying to keep up with the action. It's a bad vantage point to watch the floor, but it was a front row seat to view Grant address his team. "Are you guys really trying to screw up all that we have worked to accomplish so far?" he asked rhetorically. We looked back on that moment after the season was over. "That's probably the one time I got after them, in terms of what we did and the way we handled the situation," Grant recalled. "We had two games in a row where whatever group we had on the floor when we had a big lead kinda lost their focus. We addressed it after the game and the next time together when we watched film, we talked about it. Don't accept in victory what you wouldn't accept in defeat." Speaking of film, A. J. Schraffenberger, who shot video in the locker room after every game, was told to turn off his camera before Grant addressed the team and before he did his post-game radio interview.

It was a victory and not a defeat. With Dayton leading by 2 with 16 seconds to play, Duquesne opted to foul Obi Toppin. The eventual player of the year who had filled a highlight reel with aerobatic dunks and step-back 3-pointers calmly made the two biggest free throws of his collegiate career, and Dayton won, 73–69. Right after the game Grant talked about a game that should not have been that close: "Glad we were able to make enough plays to come out with the win," he said on radio. "But as a group we need to be more locked in and a lot better."

Hall of Fame Football Coach Mike Kelly's mantra was "It's best to patch the roof when the sun is shining," meaning you can coach a team up hard following a win without having to worry about rebuilding their confidence or getting over the pain of losing. Addressing some of the issues that arose from the Duquesne win, the Flyers prepared to host Fordham on the first day of February. The outmanned Rams tried to shorten the game, using as much clock as possible on offense, but to no avail. Fordham led for just 18 seconds in the first half, trailed by as much as 22 before Dayton posted a 70–56 final victory that was never in doubt. It was a more satisfied Coach Grant that joined me on the post-game radio show:

> I thought our guys did a good job of being locked in, in terms of taking care of the basketball. I thought they [Fordham] did a really good job of trying to control tempo and keeping the game at a manageable area. But our guys stayed the course. There was a point in the second half and you look up and they have made nine 3's, which is the only area I look at and

say we have to be better than that. I thought we did a good job of defending and rebounding, and of course when I look at 21 assists on 23 field-made baskets, that's outstanding.

Actually, I thought the offensive numbers could have been much better, as Dayton shot just 45% from the field and missed many shots that they usually make. I think that, along with the smothering defense, had me coming away feeling it was a dominant performance.

The month of February 2020 was beginning as the first half of the A-10 season was ending. Dayton was 9–0 in the A-10, riding an 11th win in a row to 20 victories. "We got nine games left in the regular season," Grant continued. "And we are in a position in which we can control our own destiny, so we gotta make sure we do the right things on and off the floor and take care of ourselves."

Two days later the Flyers moved up a notch to sixth in the AP poll, and a frequent refrain began to echo among the Flyer Faithful: "What a time to be alive!"

Moulaye Sissoko and Jordy Tshimanga

15

WE GOT THE DUB

ONE OF THE STRENGTHS OF THIS DAYTON basketball team was the fact that they were so connected at all time, on and off the floor. On a team with legitimate stars, there was no internal hierarchy. Players, coaches, managers, and trainers were all pulling in the same direction. Henry Stark was one of the senior managers. "Everyone got along and held each other accountable," he said. "They were not worried about individual accolades. Obi and Jalen were first team all-conference, but no one was jealous of them," Stark said.

On the road, I would pop in shortly before or after team meals to record Anthony's pregame interview, and I never saw the same five guys sitting together. Security guard Mike Galbraith observed the same thing as a newcomer to being around the team: "What an amazing run for me. Undefeated in all of those games, and no incidents," he told me. "They were so mature.

No challenges for me. Curfew time, I didn't have to worry about them trying to sneak out. I focused on keeping people from trying to get in."

They were a mature group, but still young guys having fun. Even the two players sitting out—Moo and Zimi—were totally engaged. Zimi made a name for himself with his celebratory leap after Obi's wind-mill dunk at Richmond, and after every game the team would celebrate the victory as Moo would announce, "We got the Dub!"—short for W—Win.

This team was endearing itself to fans not just by winning, but also by the palpable joy with which they played. Mikesell's pantomime in the background of Obi's windmill dunk at Richmond was replayed over and over on social media, giving fans a chance to also see the joyous leap by Zimi in the background. Even shooting free throws became entertaining. Jalen Crutcher was usually picked by Coach Grant to shoot technicals. With no one in the lane from either team, he would calmly bury the foul shot and then shake hands with imaginary teammates. When asked why, he explained, "That's my routine, so I stick to it."

It was a great time to be alive for the Flyer Faith-ful and the Dayton Flyers, but there were plenty of forces who were putting in time and effort in hopes of derailing both groups' dreams. After enjoying a week off following the Fordham win, the Flyers would be-gin the second half of the A-10 season hosting Saint Louis, a team that had to be still reeling from their last-second OT loss to Dayton just three weeks prior. I think the emotional gut punch led to a loss in the next game at Davidson, but then the Billikens won three in a row before getting blown out at home prior to the rematch with the Flyers. From the Saint Louis perspective, this was not about A-10 standings, this was just about beating Dayton, and they had come the closest to beating the Flyers of any team in calendar year 2020.

The game began with Dayton drawing first blood on an Obi Toppin 3-pointer, which did not bring fans to their feet but rather to their seats. On the *Anthony Grant Show* that Monday at Fricker's, Coach talked about something his wife, Chris, was hoping to initiate at Flyer home games: standing until Dayton scored its first basket. "She and the kids are on a campaign," he said. "I don't know, I'm probably letting the cat out of the bag, but she would like to have that be a tradition."

Saint Louis is usually one of the more physical teams in the A-10, but this time the Flyers were able to respond, outrebounding the Billikens in the first half and taking a 39–31 lead. Saint Louis big man Hasahn French picked up two fouls in the first half, which proved to play a huge role in the outcome. With about 13 minutes to go in the game, Saint Louis took its first lead of the second half, but French also picked up his third foul. Jalen Crutcher answered with 7 points in 3 minutes. Saint Louis didn't fold and cut the Flyer lead to 2, when French picked up his fourth foul with 6:51 to play. His fifth and final foul came with 5:11 to play, and as he exited, SLU Coach Travis Ford was livid. Rodney Chatman made three of four free throws in the final 20 seconds to ice a 71–65 win, running the Flyers, record to 21–2 and 10–0 in the Atlantic Ten. After the game, the Saint Louis radio crew of Bob Ramsey and Earl Austin were visibly upset, feeling they had been screwed by the officials. Lots of fouls were called in the game. French fouled out for SLU and Javonte Perkins was in foul trouble in the first half. Dayton's Jordy Tshimanga fouled out in just ten minutes of playing time. It had to be a bitter pill for those in and around the Billiken program to have played two very tough games against the Flyers and have nothing to show for it. In looking back, I would put the Saint Louis effort and competitiveness alongside that of Colorado and Kansas.

The bruises from the game had barely begun to fade when the Flyers were yet again faced with a "big game." I think most fans reading this have perhaps forgotten what a grind this team went through in the A-10 season. The final record makes it look easy, when, in reality, it was anything but that. VCU came to the UD Arena trailing Dayton by one game in the A-10. The Flyers then went to Saint Louis, where the Billikens trailed by one game. St. Bonaventure was just a game back when they played at the UD Arena. Duquesne and a rematch with Saint Louis were hardly breathers, with only the Fordham game one in which UD dominated from start to finish, with no fear of stumbling.

The latest "big game" would be at home against Rhode Island. Dayton was riding a 12-game winning streak, standing atop the A-10 at 10–0. Rhode Island had won 10 in a row, after dropping their A-10 opener to Richmond, and were a half-game behind the Flyers at 10–1. There are a few teams in the league that simply don't like each other, but that would be the relationship in years past between Dayton and Rhode Island, and the enmity still existed heading into this game. Adding some fuel to the fire, at least for Dayton fans, was a tweet from Jon Rothstein of CBS Sports:

> If you flip-flopped Fatts Russell and Jalen Crutcher, Dayton would be the consensus favorite to win the national title. Have to take into consideration how much easier Obi Toppin makes it for others.

The Flyer Faithful were incensed that Rothstein thought that not only was Russell a better player than Crutcher, but apparently thought Jalen was holding Dayton back, and that his numbers were due to Obi's presence. Russell was having a fine year for the Rams after a disappointing sophomore year. Dayton had split the games with URI and had crushed the Rams in Rhode Island, with Fatts shut out by Crutcher, only to have Russell go big in an overtime rematch at the UD Arena.

With much anticipation, the game began before another sellout crowd. Rhode Island won the toss, and Dayton's defense was dialed in, forcing a missed 3-pointer by Tyrese Martin. "Great start defensively by Dayton," said Brooks Hall alongside me on WHIO Radio. "Rhode Island couldn't get into their sets, couldn't get to their sweet spots, forced a tough 3, and Trey did a great job of boxing out to get the rebound." Ryan Mikesell then scored another layup at the other end. The first Rhode Island basket didn't come until 6 minutes later. In the interim Dayton had scored 17 straight, and that was the story of the game. The Flyers never trailed, leading by 14 at the half and protecting that lead for an 81–67 victory, running their winning streak to 13 in a row, 11–0 in the A-10 and now a game-and-a-half up on Rhode Island, who fell to 10–2.

There were other sidebar stories to the contest. There were seven technical fouls called in the game: four on Rhode Island (Fatts Russell, Tyrese Martin, Antwan Walker, and the bench) and three on Dayton (Trey Landers, Rodney Chatman, and the bench). Landers stepped on Fatts during a second-half scrum, and Russell needed to go to the locker room to have stitches put in a gash in his head. Someone told me afterwards they had never seen a game with seven technicals called without a fight. I said, "Because seven technicals were called there were no fights!" I thought the officials did a good job of keeping the game under control, preventing a nasty game from becoming an ugly one.

Another sidebar: the game marked the first meeting on the floor between Obi Toppin and his brother Jacob, a freshman for the Rams. They had verbally sparred a bit during the week, but the pregame hug showed it was just words. Once the game began, there was no brotherly love. Obi showed who the big brother was, to the Flyer Faithful and to the world, with a *SportsCenter* dunk in the second half. It sounded like this on radio: "Rebound Landers. Ahead to Obi. Obi, kaboom, and a foul, a foul on little brother as Obi switched hands and threw it down with the left hand." Toppin the Elder finished with 22 points and 10 rebounds, while Toppin the Younger came off the bench for 4 points and 3 rebounds. Their mom, Roni, was put in a tough position, and wore a split jersey with both sons' numbers, while spending the first half sitting with UD parents and the second half behind the Rhode Island bench. While she was there the Red Scare student body was serenading her with "Obi's better!" To which she replied, "Obi's older!"

The other noteworthy story to come out of the game came early in the first half. At the 14:43 mark, Dwayne Cohill checked into the game. There was an almost audible murmur in the crowd when he did. Cohill had not played at all against Saint Louis and saw just a minute on the floor vs. Fordham. Fans were wildly speculating that he was somehow in Coach Grant's doghouse. An accurate explanation may have come from something Keith Waleskowski had observed a few weeks prior at practice. Grant had stopped a drill and addressed Cohill, saying, "Dwayne, I am not going to beg you to give me minutes." So, surprisingly, Cohill checked in vs. Rhode Island with the game still up for grabs and gave the Flyers a big 20 minutes. He was 3-for-3 from the field, including a step-back 3-pointer after breaking Cyril Langevine's ankles. Most important of all, he had not hung his head and pouted over the previous two games. "I basically stayed ready for the moment," he told me later. "I took it as a challenge. I should have worked harder and so I did."

It was a statement game to the league, that the Flyers were the elite team, made up of elite players. Dayton would not need Fatts Russell to be a National Title contender. The roommates, the duo of Peanut Butter (Jalen Crutcher) and Jam (Obi Toppin) were rolling, as individuals, as a tandem, as teammates. In addition to Obi's 22, Crutcher added 21, including a perfect 9-for-9 from the free throw line. After the game, I asked Coach Grant for his thoughts on the pair: "They're really good players, really good individual talents, and I think they understand how to play in the framework for what we're doing, how to play with their teammates, how to make the game easier for each other. We're very fortunate to have them."

Dayton's two best players were playing their best basketball and were both being unselfish. Trey Landers and Ryan Mikesell found different ways to impact games every night. Rodney Chatman was relishing his role as a lockdown defender. Ibi Watson had become instant offense off the bench, but was more than just that, rebounding and playing defense. Dwayne Cohill and Jordy Tshimanga were providing quality bench minutes. "Toward the end of February my confidence was coming back," said Jordy after the season. "Coach Grant was great. He wants to do what's best for everyone. He told me to be patient. Don't rush it. My teammates, and even the fans were supportive of me through the whole process."

The praises were flowing in from media all over the country, and fans everywhere in Flyer Nation. But not only did this team, in the words of Coach Grant, "trust the process," but they embraced the process, enjoying every step on the road, celebrating and savoring every victory.

Like Moo said: "We got the Dub!"

**Crowd at Fricker's for
Anthony Grant Radio Show**

16

SURVIVING THE DOG DAYS

THE LAST HALF OF FEBRUARY ARE THE dog days of the basketball season, akin to August in baseball. The grind of a long season, and in recent years, a preseason that begins during the summer, takes its toll on a team. I often hear fans scoff at the notion, as they remember some magical vigor they all possessed as a nineteen- or twenty-year-old. The reality is there is a greater mental drain than a physical one affecting the players, and in some cases even the staff. With the exception of a week in May and another week in early August, they have been around each other on an almost daily basis. Practice, individual workouts, film sessions, walk-throughs, travel, and those things called college classes all take a cumulative effect on the energy of each person as well as the collective group. I can remember teams in the past hitting some type of invisible wall, especially freshmen who are playing in the biggest number of meaningful games in their lives. In mid-to-late February, great teams will stumble, good teams will fade, and bad teams collapse. At that time of year, one is either counting the days until the season is over or making the days count.

Dayton, obviously, was in position to make the days count. After beating Rhode Island, it looked like it would take a huge letdown for the Flyers to not take home the regular season title, given head-to-head edges over the other contenders—Rhode Island, Richmond, Saint Louis, Duquesne, and St. Bonaventure.

There were no more "first place on the line" games left on the schedule, but there were plenty of chances for a so-called bad loss. The first of these came after the home win over Rhode Island, a road game at UMass. I've already written disparagingly about the home court at LaSalle. There are other venues in the A-10 of a similar size. St. Bonaventure is a great place for a college basketball game because of the passion of their fans. When Saint Joseph's is good, they are hard to beat at Hagan Arena. George Washington's student body can make the Smith Center tough on visitors, and the same holds true for Davidson. VCU's gym (not an arena) is the second-loudest to the UD Arena. Saint Louis, Richmond, Rhode Island, and George Mason all have good places to play. Fordham's Rose Hill gym is old and tiny but is always packed with Dayton fans. Pittsburgh is an easy trip for the Flyers Faithful, so no matter what facility Duquesne uses, it has a friendly feel. And then there is UMass.

The University of Dayton's first game in the Atlantic Ten was at UMass on January 6, 1996. UMass was the No. 1 team in the nation and the Mullins Center was packed. Dayton was competitive for the first few minutes before losing 78–58. The late Chris Daniels, however, had a solid game, scoring 20 points.

He then delivered one of the best lines ever in the post-game press conference. When asked how it felt to go up against national player-of-the-year candidate Marcus Camby, he replied, "I don't know. I don't have cable."

In recent years the Mullins Center has been nearly vacant for Flyer visits. Two thousand people in an arena that seats 9,493 looks like spit in the ocean. It also serves as a hockey arena with ice under the basketball floor, which means it's not only empty but it's cold, with coaches' instructions echoing through the building and only occasionally muffled by music and polite applause.

Paid attendance on this Saturday afternoon was listed at 5,030. There were not 5,030 people in the seats. However, just as they had in their A-10 opening win over LaSalle, the Flyers took care of business. It was not a dominating performance, but when you are Superman you get everyone's best shot of kryptonite. Dayton led by 5 at the half, but late in the second half UMass went on a run to cut the Flyer lead to 4 with 14.5 seconds to play. Jalen Crutcher then calmly made two free throws, and following a UMass miss, Dwyane Cohill, buried on the bench just a few weeks before, iced the game with two more free throws and a 71–63 win. The game was also a matchup of the reigning A-10 Rookie of the Year Obi Toppin, who led UD with 19 points, and the eventual 2020 A-10 Rookie of the Year Tre Mitchell, who had 26 and 10 rebounds. "You've got to be able to win when you don't play well," said Anthony Grant in his post-game radio interview. "And today was one of those where we didn't necessarily play well, but we found a way to win." Dayton's winning streak was extended to 14 as the Flyers improved to 23–2 overall, and 12–0 in conference.

While Coach Grant may not have been impressed with his team's performance, Dayton moved up to No. 5 in the AP poll released that Monday. That evening the Flyer Faithful gathered at Fricker's on Woodman Drive in Dayton for the *Anthony Grant Show* on WHIO Radio from 7–8:00. The event had always been well attended in the previous two seasons. But as this season progressed and the wins mounted, the numbers swelled beyond the capacity of the back room reserved for the event. David Gasper was one of the regulars in attendance. "Our group of six would send one couple to Fricker's to reserve a table at 4:00 to 4:30 each Monday," he said. "They would stay and guard the table. If they arrived by 5:00 they had a good chance of getting shut out. Our joke was the line from *Jaws*. 'We're gonna need a bigger boat.' The crowds were awesome!"

Anthony would usually play his cards close to the vest during these shows. He would fully answer my questions and those from the audience, but he never revealed any insights that could give a future opponent an edge or provide any bulletin board material. He made his biggest impact on the crowd after the show was over. Each week he made it a point to greet every single person in attendance, going table to table, and even thanking those who stood in the hallway.

Anthony Grant had endeared himself to Dayton fans as a player and now had won over even the skeptics as a coach. He had not faced any resistance on campus and in the university community. It started with his very first game, when he shook hands with every person sitting at the scorer's table. He did, and still does the same with the security guards who work the floor.

That same affection for Grant lingers at VCU, where he coached the Rams from 2006–2009, going to the NCAA Tournament twice, including an upset win over Duke in his first season. The game day staff all welcome him back, many of whom went out of their way to say hi. He and the Flyers were not so warmly greeted by the current VCU fans.

The preseason picks to win the A-10 were now focusing on trying to get a first-round bye in the A-10 tournament. There were whispers that the team's seniors were in a funk, that their final year was not what they had hoped it would be. Coach Mike Rhoades was giving more playing time to young players like freshman Bones Hyland, who came off the bench in the first meeting with the Flyers to score 16.

He was in the starting lineup, while preseason first team All-Conference selection Marcus Evans sat the entire game with an injury. The personnel may have changed somewhat for the Rams, but the game plan had not. Defend and rebound and try and turn Dayton mistakes into easy baskets. While both teams preferred a wide open, up-tempo game, neither defense allowed it, and the Flyers had a 36–29 lead at halftime.

Josh Postorino was working with me on radio, and we were both waiting for an offensive explosion in the second half, like we had seen in the first win against VCU, but it never came. Stingy Rams defense combined with a Dayton offense that was just not clicking to create a physical grind. A pair of Jalen Crutcher free throws with 8:15 to play extended the Flyers lead to 9. Two minutes later Ibi Watson missed a 3 and then fouled Vince Williams as he completed the fast break for the Rams with a layup. Williams made the ensuing free throw and the UD lead was down to just 2. To call what happened next a turning point in the season would be too strong of a statement, but how the Flyers finished this game may have defined them as much as some of Obi's aerial acts and Crutcher and Watson's offensive bursts. Trey Landers hit a free throw to increase the lead to 3. Crutcher then rebounded a miss by Hyland and was fouled. He made both of his free throws to put Dayton up 5. Crutcher added two more free throws and Cohill made one of two, but Malik Crowfield hit a 3 for the Rams and Dayton led 58–54 heading into the under-4 time out.

The previous season Dayton lost some close games like this, on the road and at home against VCU, George Mason, Rhode Island, and Mississippi State. However, this team now had fresher legs and a mature resolve to step up and make plays. Coming out of the time-out, De'Riante Jenkins was fouled. He was VCU's best free throw shooter and one of the best in the A-10. But he made just one of two, and Obi Toppin scored on a short jumper to bump the Flyer lead back to 5 with three minutes to play. It was Dayton's final field goal of the night. With 22 seconds to go, Dayton led by just 3, but Dwayne Cohill and Jalen Crutcher combined to go 4-for-4 from the line to ice a 66–61 win. Dayton was 24–2, 13–0 in the A-10, while VCU dropped to 7–6 in league play. Crutcher was a perfect 8-for-8 from the line in the second half and finished with a team-high 18 points. Dayton made just six field goals in the second half and just one 3-pointer, but held the Rams to 36.8% from the field.

"It wasn't a pretty night offensively," Coach Grant said in his post-game radio interview. "We had to find ways to win the game." The victory was a sweet one, given the environment and the opponent. "Our guys handled adversity, and adversity came at us in a lot of different ways tonight," he continued. "It was a very hard-fought game. They do a great job of disrupting what you are trying to do offensively. They had a really good game plan." Dayton had better talent, however, and certainly had more to play for in terms of charting its post-season path, but what truly emerged was the culmination of a culture that had its seeds in the previous year and then was nurtured through the summer and with every step along the way this season. "We got some great minutes from a variety of guys either in the starting lineup or off the bench," Grant went on to say. "It was to me a great team effort and we showed a lot of resiliency, a lot of character. What we like to call being 'Dayton Strong.'"

Josh Postorino worked that game with me at VCU and before that the game at Richmond as well as the neutral site games vs. Saint Mary's and Colorado. He also attended several games home and away in which he did not broadcast. He stayed on top of what was happening from his home base in Phoenix, but his episodic viewing of the growth of the team gave him a unique perspective. "I thought after you and I did the game in Phoenix vs. Saint Mary's and we totally dismantled them, we were going to be special," Josh told me later. "The team wasn't too far from the Maui travel and had to fly back out west. Everything was set up for an excuse loss. Saint Mary's was good and we made it look like they didn't belong on the same floor. Focus was tremendous. Saint Mary's beat Arizona State 96–56 a week later."

My biggest takeaway from the win at VCU was how much more mentally tough this team had become. They won a game when things did not come easily, especially at the offensive end. Postorino's background as a player, but also as an assistant coach under Oliver Purnell at Dayton, Clemson, and DePaul, and with Brian Gregory at Georgia Tech gave him an X and O appreciation of Dayton's offense. Postorino observed,

I think the staff did a great job of sticking with their system of spacing the floor running their continuous ball screen offense "p game" [passing game]. They could have scrapped it this season after two mediocre offensive years. It really fit their personnel because of not having a back to the basket guy. They had two elite players involved in a high percentage of ball-screens. Obi was the best in the country at setting the ball-screen and playing options off of it. Jalen was right at the top in the country of using the ball-screen and making decisions with the ball. That high level of basketball talent hasn't been seen at Dayton. Scoochie was great off the screen, but they did not have an Obi. I also think what they ran didn't make Trey and Ryan have to create offense. It just came to them.

The team left Richmond having completed two kind of sweeps—both games in that city vs. the Richmond Spiders first, and then now VCU—and taking both games vs. the Rams. The A-10 standings were an afterthought now. This team did not just want to win the Atlantic Ten, they wanted to dominate it, something Anthony Grant had promised in his introductory press conference.

The Flyers had the talent, the grit, the game plan, the maturity, and the desire to win, but they still had to face opponents who had a chance for a marquee win if they could knock off the Flyers. One such team was Duquesne. The Dukes came to the UD Arena for a rematch on Saturday afternoon, February 22, 2020. I spent the morning getting some tickets squared away for my family. My oldest daughter, Lauren, was coming down from Cleveland with her fiancé Nate (who had called me right after the Colorado loss to ask for my blessing, taking some sting away from what now seemed like a long-ago distant memory disappointment). It was going to be his first UD game, but Lauren had been going to games since she was a toddler and once even ran out on the floor at the end of the court to chastise Xavier cheerleaders.

I probably could not have picked a better game for them to attend. Another sellout crowd was amped up, and the two teams traded threes to start the game, setting the tone for a back-and-forth battle. Dayton's biggest lead in the half was just 2, and Duquesne's was 4 when Obi scored off of a dump-off from Rodney Chatman to end the half. The Flyers trailed 38–36, only the second time they had trailed at the half all season, the other time being at Saint Louis. However, there was no vibe within the crowd, and certainly coming off the team, that the Flyers were in any way in trouble.

The second half began with Ryan Mikesell scoring off a feed from Obi to tie the game at 38. Obi then finished a fast break with a thunderous dunk, jumping off two feet just inside the foul line to give Dayton the lead. Duquesne answered with a short jumper by Lamar Norman. A minute later Obi Toppin hit the second of two free throws to start the kind of burst that had become a trademark of this Dayton team. When Trey Landers had a stick-back off of an offensive rebound, Dayton led 66–49 with just under 9 minutes to play. The Flyers had outscored the Dukes 26–9 in an 8-minute stretch. Jalen Crutcher was the catalyst again, scoring 13 points and assisting on a 3 by Obi and a dunk by Obi that gave Toppin 1,000 points in his Flyer career. With his first dunk of the game he broke his own single season school record (84) and he finished the game with 28 points, shooting 11–16 from the field and 3–5 from 3-point range. Crutcher finished with 17, all in the second half. After the game in his interview heard on WHIO Radio and throughout the Arena, Coach Grant praised his team's determination. "They decided to come out in the second half and impose their will on the game as a unit," he said. "As a team we have a chance to do some special things if guys are locked in the way they were in the second half." The cream rose to the top in that second-half explosion in the form of the roommates, Peanut Butter (Jalen) and Jam (Obi), but Grant marveled at how they fit in as pieces of the whole. "We have great teammates," he continued. "Obi, what he is able to do speaks for itself. But I think in that locker room, the way guys all get along together with each other, it's really a special group."

Perhaps the best praise and most objective analysis of Dayton that day came from Duquesne Coach Keith Dambrot in his comments to the Pittsburgh media:

> They are a "spurty" team. If you don't score and match their ability to score you are not going to win. Everybody talks about Toppin, and he's great, but Crutcher is the one for them. When they are in trouble, Crutcher makes plays. If you allow them to be fluid and throw the ball from side-to-side, you're going to get your brains beat in. They are one of the most fluid teams in the country if

you allow them to be. I judge things by what I've seen over the last thirty years. As far as system, coaching, understanding his players, he could be National Coach of the Year. It's just my opinion. They play hard for him, they're smart, the sum of the parts is a lot greater than the individual pieces. That's no disrespect for them individually, they got a lot of really good players. There's a lot of guys on that team that people don't know how good they are. Trey Landers. Obi's so good, nobody hears about Trey. He's one of the toughest guys in the league. Mikesell. You could argue he's the best winner. Just a winning, unselfish guy. And then there's Crutcher. You can go down the line to guys like Cohill, playing their roles. He's just done a good job of getting them to buy in to what they do.

National Coach of the Year. Maybe Keith Dambrot can also say, "I told you so."

**Anthony Grant and House of Bread
Director, Melodie Bennett**

17

WHAT A TIME TO BE ALIVE

WITH THE REST OF THE COMPETITION IN the rearview mirror, the Flyers' focus now was just to win every game. Gordon Gecko said, "Greed is good" in the movie *Wall Street*. And this Flyer team was getting greedy in the best possible way. After taking care of business at VCU and at home against Duquesne, Dayton moved up a notch to fourth in the AP poll on Monday, February 24, 2020. There was no chance to celebrate at the *Anthony Grant Show* at Fricker's, as for the second week in a row, Monday was a travel day, Dayton heading to George Mason for a Tuesday night game vs. the Patriots.

Dayton fans did not need to gather in one spot to be absolutely giddy about the team's success. John Bedell hosted *Flyer Feedback* from Flanagan's after home games along with a rotation of former Flyers: Keith Waleskowski, Brooks Hall, Nate Green, and Rex Gardecki. John then was joined by John Tisdell in the WHIO Studios for *Flyer Feedback* following away games. "What was that line the fanbase kept echoing throughout the season as Dayton kept climbing the Top 25 rankings and piling up the wins and accolades? 'What a time to be alive!'" Bedell recalled after the season. "The Flyer Faithful kept pinching themselves making sure it was all real. 'Just don't wake me up from this dream season,' one *Flyer Feedback* regular kept telling me at Flanagan's Pub after games. It's why we (and many others) started referring to it on the show, maybe only half-jokingly, as 'the season of dreams.'"

While it was a "season of dreams" for fans, it was a season of vision for the players, staff, and most notably, Coach Anthony Grant. His vision for the program was manifesting itself with on-court success and an impact on the community off the court. The painful memories of the Memorial Day tornadoes, the Oregon District shootings, and the death of officer Del Rio were eased by a team that played together and cared about each other. It was as if their love for the game and their love for their teammates was shining a bright light on a city that had witnessed such dark moments only months earlier. John Bedell saw it not just as the host of *Flyer Feedback*, but in his role as a reporter for WHIO-TV. "After the tumultuous 2019 the Dayton region experienced, I think the season the Flyers had was a nice escape for a lot of folks," he said. "It provided a time for two hours a night, twice a week, from Thanksgiving to early March, where they could forget about their troubles and get lost in the fun of UD basketball. It was a distraction that brought a lot of joy to a lot of folks who love the Flyers. A chance for the Dayton Flyers to lift their 'Dayton Strong' community, our community, after a tough time. They sure made us proud."

Barry Hall of Champion Auto had seen his Greater Old North Dayton Business Area devastated by the tornadoes but found solace in the view from his seat at the UD Arena. "Everybody needed something to bring some joy in their lives," Hall said. "This team comes along. Obi, Anthony, Jalen, and Trey, growing up around here. He is a wonderful young man. As much as I loved the Don May era and the team that Archie had with just seven guys, this team is right up there. It honestly looked like a team and they were having fun."

Coach Grant had stuck with his vision from day one, and it was paying off. He could have said, "I told you so," but that's not his style. Bedell remembered *Flyer Feedback* in that rough first year transition. "Here's what I'll say about the changing attitudes toward Anthony Grant over his first three years at Dayton," he told me. "Flyer fans wanting the head coach fired before he's spent three years on the job seems to have become a rite of passage for the steward of the program these days." John was referring to February of 2014 when Archie Miller, then in his third year, had seen UD go 1–5 to start the A-10 season. "We had one caller who dialed us up that night with his shortlist of names to replace Miller at the ready," John said. "This guy broadcasted his wish list that included then-Akron Head Coach Keith Dambrot and Bruce Pearl—who was out of a coaching job and working in TV because his show-cause penalty hadn't expired yet. But that didn't seem to matter. People were ready to cut bait with Miller."

Shortly thereafter, the Flyers went on a run that didn't stop until the Elite Eight of the NCAA Tournament in March. No one brought up firing Archie Miller again. However, some fans didn't even wait for Grant to complete his first season to question his hiring. Bedell continued,

> I found myself thinking we had en-
> tered another silly season on the
> Dayton hoops beat when some sec-
> tions of the Dayton fanbase seemed
> convinced it was time to sell their
> Anthony Grant stock just nine games
> into his stint as the head man at UD.
> I mean, that had to be a land speed
> record for such a loss of faith. You
> know, a foundation might not look
> like much as it stands alone on a
> construction site—but any foreman
> worth their salt knows how crucial
> that base is to the success of the
> building that will eventually sit on
> top of it. Beginning in late spring
> 2017, Grant metaphorically placed
> every brick and block perfectly level
> against a guiding mason's line—sus-
> pended ever taut above each new
> course. Grant never veered from his
> blueprint along the way.

Associate Head Coach Anthony Solomon had
been there since day one. "I was impressed with
Coach Grant," he told me. "We didn't compromise
our principles that first year. He stayed with his vision
for what the program was to be all about."

For players like Obi Toppin, buying into Grant's
vision was the key. "He was like another father," Toppin said. "He put in the effort to make sure that I was
good. He wanted everyone to succeed. He was pushing me every day when I sat out my first year."

With doubters and nay-sayers silent, the 4th-ranked

Dayton Flyers need not look over their shoulders but could focus on the next task at hand. George Mason had beaten the Flyers the previous season at the UD Arena, one of those losses that still stuck in Anthony Grant's craw, but this Mason squad had seen its roster depleted by a double whammy—graduation of their all-conference point guard Otis Livingston and then the unforeseen injuries to Ian Boyd and Justin Kier, who had been the A-10's Chris Daniels Award winner as the most improved player in the league. Nevertheless, like a wounded animal, GMU prepared to try and knock off the kings of the A-10 hill. As expected, the Patriots slowed the game down and tried to get physical and frustrate the Flyers. Dayton kept its poise and had a 30–25 lead at the half. George Mason then came out strong in the second half and took a 2-point lead with 13:49 to go. Thirty seconds later, Ibi Watson hit a 3, and the Flyers never trailed again, winning 62–55 despite only going 3–8 from the free throw line down the stretch. Watson finished with 9 points, but they were the biggest 9 points of the game, all coming after the Patriots took the lead in the second half. It was a typical Ibi performance, as he showed throughout the season the ability to come into games and create an offensive spark without being a high-volume shooter.

While the Flyer Faithful who showed up in Fairfax, Virginia, hoping to see a Dayton rout may have been disappointed, Coach Grant was not concerned at all about style points as he joined me for the post-game radio interview, "What this team has been able to do, able to answer every bell up to this point in the season," he said. "We have a chance with three games left to do some historic things. This is fun. It's creating some memories. We got to make sure we enjoy that and keep things in perspective."

Dayton was now 26–2, winners of 17 in a row, and were heading home to host Davidson on Friday with a win clinching the Atlantic Ten title outright. "That's the number one goal is to try and win a championship," Grant continued. "We want to be selfish. We want to make sure we take care of winning it outright."

It was not just a sell-out crowd, but a festival atmosphere at the UD Arena that Friday. The game was being nationally televised on ESPN, with Dick Vitale on hand. He bantered with the crowd and posed for pictures. Vitale had put ESPN on the map in its early days and even though he was working fewer games, Dayton fans were anxious to see and hear him bestow his blessings on the Flyers. Yes, Dayton was 26–2. Yes, the Flyers had won 17 in a row. Yes, Obi Toppin was a Player-of-the-Year candidate and a lock to be a first-round NBA draft pick. Yes, Anthony Grant was a Coach-of-the-Year candidate. But what did Dickie V. think?

The Flyers could not have handed the ESPN crew a better script. The reigning A-10 Player-of-the-Year Jón-Axel Guðmundsson hit a 3 to open the game for Davidson. Jalen Crutcher answered with a 3. Kellan Grady, also a preseason first team all-conference pick, hit a short jumper to put the Wildcats back up by two. Rodney Chatman nailed a 3, and the Flyers never trailed the rest of the game. Obi Toppin hit a 3 at the 2-minute mark to put Dayton up 20, and Davidson was only able to cut it to 18 before halftime. In addition to Dayton's offense shooting a blistering 69% from the field while holding Davidson to just 37%, Vitale came on the video boards during a time-out in the first half to announce that ESPN's *College GameDay* was coming to campus the following Saturday.

In the second half, the Wildcats heated up to shoot 58% from the field while making 6-for-11 3-pointers. But Dayton surpassed its first half shooting, hitting 76% of its shots. It was the second-best shooting performance in school history, surpassed only by 77% against an overmatched Southern University team in 1986. Obi Toppin added to his national stardom, scoring 23 points, making 10-for-11 from the field and 3-for-4 from behind the arc, while pulling down 12 rebounds and dishing out 4 assists. His 4 dunks in the game put him at 96 on the season and surpassed Chris Wright for the UD career dunk record with 179. Afterward he came over to press row and leaned in to shake Dick Vitale's hand. I saw that, and all I could think was, *Awesome, baby!* Dayton had played two Friday games on ESPN. Those Friday nights were meant to showcase the A-10, and the Flyers did their part, giving the nation a thrilling overtime win at Saint Louis and now this clinic in offensive efficiency.

The Flyers improved to 27–2, the win streak moved to 18–0, and with the 82–67 final victory they were outright A-10 regular season champs, regardless of what happened in the final two games. Coach Grant used his post-game radio program to address the crowd at the UD Arena: "I can't thank you guys enough for the energy you brought tonight," he said, his voice hoarse from coaching up his team. "Our guys were really locked in. I thought it was a heckuva game. We were not going to be denied tonight. Our guys came out and we fought. Thank you for all the support and we still got more to do."

I had asked AD Neil Sullivan before the game, if the team would cut down the nets as A-10 Champs if they won. He said it was entirely up to Coach Grant, and he had no feel which way the coach was thinking. At the time, I thought they should have cut down the nets so as to savor every accomplishment along the way, but I can't argue with the coach's decision, especially in light of what then happened the following Saturday.

The next day was a rare Saturday off during the basketball season, and my son took advantage of that and had me help him move. Before I did that, I went to the House of Bread early in the morning. The House of Bread feeds hungry people a hot, nutritious, lunch 365 days a year with no questions asked. It is an organization that I have become actively involved with, volunteering throughout the year and using my platform to raise awareness, encouraging others to volunteer and make donations. Coach Grant's wife, Chris, had heard me talk about it and expressed interest in volunteering sometime. She contacted me earlier in the week and asked if she could volunteer and bring some friends on Saturday. I told her what time to arrive and what to expect. Before I went to pick up the U-Haul for the move, I drove to the House of Bread to meet Chris and to introduce her to Executive Director Melodie Bennett. When I arrived, her friends were already there and working busily in the kitchen. Soon thereafter an SUV pulled up and Chris Grant got out of the passenger side, with Anthony Grant exiting from the driver's seat. The man who had just won the Atlantic Ten Championship outright the night before was celebrating by volunteering at a "soup kitchen." I introduced him to Melodie, gave them a quick tour, and when I left to go help my son move, he was happily carving turkeys for lunch that day.

The dream season kept getting better for Dayton fans as the AP poll came out on Monday, and the Flyers had moved up to third in the nation, trailing only Kansas and Gonzaga. Fricker's was overflowing with

Flyer fans, many of whom could not hear the *Anthony Grant Radio Show*, but simply waited in the main dining area to greet the coach afterward. Several time zones away, Josh Postorino was feeling the Flyer Fever rise to almost as hot as the Arizona desert near Phoenix. "When Dayton made the top 25, people started to notice, but then when you make the top 10 I think you become more national," Josh recalled. "I started getting comments on my Dayton shirts while I was hiking and running on trails. Obi contributed to that the most when he was in conversation for POY. He was on Scott Van Pelt's show every night! On the West Coast his show is primetime for us."

UD Sports Information Director Doug Hauschild was deftly handling national media requests while still giving the local media access to Coach Grant and the players. "So easy to work with," he described the experience. "Obi was Obi. He was playful and genuine. My only issue with having him at a press gathering was that after he was done he would hang around and try to make his teammates crack up and would photo-bomb them." The maturity of the team added to the overall picture of the program that was being painted for the world. "Ryan and Trey were not just leaders on the floor, they were leaders in dealing with the media," Hauschild continued. "They were thoughtful, not clichéd in their comments and were able to offer third-person insights to the things that Obi and Jalen were doing. As a team, they were more interested in talking about each other than they were in talking about themselves. Obi was uncomfortable getting all the attention, so he would make it a point to bring a teammate with him when asked to do a post-game TV interview."

When I woke up on the Friday of the Davidson game, I had a sore throat. In thirty-nine years of calling Flyer games, I have learned to read my body, and I knew I had something coming on. It's a rare season that I do not have some type of respiratory issue with a nagging cough and stuffed-up nose. I had a bad cold earlier at the start of the A-10 season in Philadelphia and thought that would be my one bout of the year. However, the sore throat prompted me to call my doctor and try to nip things in the bud. I was taking antibiotics and drinking tea as I traveled with the team to Rhode Island for what would be the final true road game of the year. There are many things that impressed me about this Dayton squad. Looking inside that 27–2 record at the time was an 8–0 mark away from the Arena in league play. It is my opinion that the hardest thing to do in team sports is to win a college basketball conference road game. In 2018–19, Dayton had a spectacular 7–2 in A-10 road games, and this squad had taken it a step further.

Upon arrival in Rhode Island, we went straight to the Ryan Center for a shootaround before checking into the hotel. Trainer Mike Mulcahey had noticed my coughing and overall miserable countenance and gave me some cough drops and antihistamines. He then called Dr. James, one of the team doctors and asked what he should do about having a sick radio guy around the team. Dr. James suggested I wear a mask, and Mike asked me if I would. I agreed and he handed me an N95 mask which I wore during practice and on the bus to the hotel. Coach Grant just looked at me, grinned and shook his head. For my part, I felt like I was wearing the "cone of shame," like a dog who had been to the vet, but I did not want to jeopardize the team. How would I feel if this dream season was derailed because of me?

After practice, Brooks Hall and I grabbed a late-night dinner after checking into the hotel, and I self-medicated with some clam chowder. I don't know if it helps with a cold, but I like it. Brooks had been with me on the same trip two years ago, when Dayton had lost to the Rams on their Senior Night, and they clinched the A-10 title outright. Now the A-10 Champion Flyers would try to pay back Rhode Island by spoiling the night for their seniors, notably guard Jeff Dowtin and big man Cyril Langevine. That game in 2018 saw the Flyers trailing by just two at the half, only to be blown out by the Rams in the second half. Rhode Island was a senior-laden team, ranked 18th in the country and had lost just one A-10 game. Not only did Dayton not play the spoiler that evening, but the 81–56 loss had dropped UD to 13–15 overall, with two games left in the regular season. A losing season seemed to be inevitable. I can vividly remember being showered by confetti and large pieces of glitter that fell from the ceiling at game's end. The Rams were still celebrating on the floor when Coach Grant came out to press row for his post-game radio interview. I could feel the steam coming off him, as even though URI was a better team that night, and that season, the sting of losing was exacerbated by the scene on the floor. I was picking glitter out of my briefcase for weeks.

Now Dayton came in, already wearing the crown, but with a chance to still be a spoiler of the Rams Senior Night. It was also round two of Fatts Russell vs. Jalen Crutcher as to who was the best point guard in the A-10. In the first meeting at the UD Arena, where tempers flared to a near brawl and seven technical fouls were called, Fatts had 19 points, but needed 18 shots to get them, and hit only one 3-pointer. He also left with three stitches in his head after being stepped on in a scrum involving Rodney Chatman and Trey Landers. The rancor had palpably carried over as the game began. Dayton coaches had spent the previous evening, and in film sessions that day emphasizing the need to hold Rhode Island to just one shot. Every defensive stand needed to end with a rebound.

Roni Toppin had her split UD/URI jersey on, with both of her boys' names and numbers, and again split time sitting behind each respective bench. Dayton took an early 11–7 lead, and then opened up some daylight on an Obi slam. Four minutes later Jordy Tshimanga hit back-to-back baskets to put Dayton up 25–14, prompting a 30-second Rams time-out. A pair of Fatts Russell free throws cut the Flyers lead to 5 with 7:30 to play in the half. Obi assisted on a basket by Ibi Watson, Jhery Matos dropped off a pass to Obi for a layup, and he then dunked to put UD back up by 11. The defense then yielded just one free throw by Jeff Dowtin the final 3minutes of the half, and Dayton went to the locker room leading 46–30. Fatts Russell was held to 6 points on 2-for-8 shooting from the field and was hit with a technical foul. Rodney Chatman and Dwayne Cohill had combined to frustrate him, while Jalen Crutcher did his thing, leading Dayton with 12 points and a pair of assists.

The poised and confident Flyers never let up and turned the second half into a rout, sending most Rhode Island fans home before the seniors could exit late for their curtain call. The Rams got within 12 two minutes into the half, but then Dayton pulled away, and when walk-on Christian Wilson hit a 3 for the final UD basket, the Flyers had a convincing 27-point win, 84–57.

Wilson was a great example of how each player bought into their role on the team:

> I just have a deep love for the game
> of basketball. I grew up watching
> Dayton basketball, since I am from

here. I tried out freshman year and
unfortunately didn't make it, partly
due to my class schedule being in en-
gineering. So, I took that year to get
better to try out again and make it
the following year.

Christian had reached out to Brooks Hall after that
first year for advice on how he needed to prepare.
The experience of being a part of a special team was
an impactful one. Wilson remarked, "I have learned a
lot from the coaching staff about the game of basketball. There is a lot more to it than I would have ever
thought if I did not have this opportunity to play."

Fellow walk-on Camron Greer had punctuated a
Dayton win at Rhode Island the previous season with
a late three, and he talked to me about his experience
as a Flyer. "I love the game of basketball. That's all
you dream of as a kid: to play the sport you love at
the highest levels. Though my route to playing Division I basketball was much different from others, I
still made sure it happened at any cost," he explained.
"Not many people can say they've had an experience
such as this one. Those are the people I do it for. All
the hours I spent in the gym up until the point felt
worth it; not only for me, but for my family, friends,
and supporters as well."

The subdued exit by the Rhode Island players after
the game was such a sharp contrast to two years ago,
as Coach Grant made the same walk out to press row
to join me on the radio. As they had in the first meeting at the UD Arena, the Flyers had held the Rams
to a paltry 29% shooting from the field, "I thought
we were really good defensively," he said. "I thought
our guys were able to take the challenge of coming
in here on Senior Night, against a team, in my opin-

ion, that is an NCAA [tournament] caliber team. A lot of emotion, a sold-out building. Our guys did a good job defensively." And the point of emphasis in preparation for the game, paid off in results. "In the first meeting they got 14 offensive rebounds," he continued. "I thought for the most part we controlled the boards. We outrebounded them by 11 tonight which is good." Leading the effort on the glass was Trey Landers who matched his 14 points with 14 rebounds. "He was incredible," Grant commented. "In the second half there were some balls that were bouncing around there, and you see him keep going up and up and up, he just kept getting them and wasn't going to be denied on the glass tonight." Perhaps Coach Grant was remembering the confetti and the dancing of two years previous when he said, "We're going to enjoy this. This is a great win for us and then we're going to get prepared for GW on Saturday night. It's our Senior Night. It will be a chance to go 18–0 for the first time in league history. A lot for us to play for, we are going to be excited to get back in front of our fans, and send our seniors off the right way."

Just one game left in the regular season and even the most pessimistic of the Flyer Faithful could not envision this team stubbing their toe. A No. 1 seed in the NCAA Tournament was looking likely. The team could add the Atlantic Ten tournament title to the regular season championship. The Flyers had won nineteen in a row. Surely, they could win six in a row in the NCAA Tournament. There was a perfect spot high above Blackburn Court to hang a National Championship banner in the UD Arena.

What a time to be alive!

I quickly packed up the radio gear and headed for the bus, where I put my N95 face mask on for the bus ride, and then the charter plane ride home, after which, I threw it in my briefcase, thinking I would never need it again.

**Anthony Grant cuts down the net
following season finale**

18

AND THEN IT WAS OVER

THE CELEBRATION FOLLOWING THE regular-season-ending win over George Washington spilled over into the next day. The awards banquet was held Sunday morning at the Steam Plant in Downtown Dayton. Players and their families were joined by the coaches, staff, athletic department personnel, as well as some boosters. I was the emcee of the event, which had more of a forward-moving feel than a recap of the season. The team had last lost a game the week before Christmas, and it seemed even longer than that. Most of the conversations swirled around potential NCAA Tournament sites. Many were hoping the Flyers would be sent to Cleveland, and I had contacted my future son-in-law, Nate, about having a team function at his pinball parlor, Super Electric in the Gordon Square area on the city's west side.

Coach Grant talked briefly, and the awards were

handed out:

2019–20 UNIVERSITY OF DAYTON MEN'S BASKETBALL AWARDS

White-Allen Most Valuable Player
Jalen Crutcher & Obi Toppin
Alex Schoen Free Throw Percentage
Jalen Crutcher
John L. Macbeth Scholar-Athlete
Jordy Tshimanga
Dr. George Rau Spirit Award
Ryan Mikesell
"Shorty" Sharpenter Top Rebounder
Obi Toppin
Chris Daniels Memorial Award
Trey Landers
Thomas M. Luppe Memorial Award
Ibi Watson
Steve McElvene Best Defender Award
Rodney Chatman & Trey Landers
Uhl Family Endowed Scholarship
Jordy Tshimanga
James G. and Purcell S. Palmer Scholarship
Trey Landers

That afternoon I participated in a celebrity chicken wing eating contest for charity at Blind Bob's in the Oregon District. I took my time and enjoyed my wings but did raise some money. The conversation was all about the Flyers. We were sitting just outside the scene of the carnage that took place there in August, and the basketball team had helped not just that neighborhood, but the entire city heal over the ensuing months. Jeff Gonya and his wife, Leslie, live in the Oregon District. "I noticed after Maui, if people saw you wear something with the logo, they would start talking about basketball," he told me. "Oregon District is not a big sports area, but the bars would be showing the Flyers games on TV and non-fans were even talking about them." In addition to running their bed and breakfast and wine shop there, Leslie has her own travel agency and was preparing to take sixty-one Flyer Faithful to Brooklyn that week for the Atlantic Ten Championship.

Another packed house was on hand for the final *Anthony Grant Show* of the season that Monday at Fricker's, and as usual Coach Grant thanked everyone after the show for coming, not just that evening, but for their support throughout the season. Dave Gaspar was one of the regulars each week. "It was a season of magic and often stunned disbelief," he recalled. "It was if you watched the game and then asked yourself, 'Did that just happen? Was that dunk real? Did they just blow that team away?' I have so many OMG moments this year. It was incredible. Wish it could happen again."

The final *Anthony Grant Radio Show* of the season was followed the next day by release of the Atlantic 10 post-season awards. There was really very little drama, as Obi Toppin was named the Player of the Year and Anthony Grant the Coach of the Year. Jalen Crutcher joined Obi on the First Team All-A-10 squad and Trey Landers was named Third Team All-Conference. For the second year in a row, Ryan Mikesell was named to the All-Academic team in the league. The only slight I saw was Rodney Chatman being left off the All-Defensive team. I figured that would only fuel his fire that week in Brooklyn, and I looked for him to deliver some shut-down performances.

I was, however, particularly proud of Trey Landers. The league coaches saw what an impact he made in so many ways. His journey from a freshman who rarely saw the floor to gaining All-Conference honors as a senior was a testament to his work ethic and the leadership he showed. Although he didn't get much playing time that first year, I can remember Archie Miller telling me, "If someone came and watched practice, they would have no idea that Trey didn't play much. He approached practice every day as if he was a starter."

Trey had his doubts about staying with the program when Archie left, but his trust in Anthony Grant, and then the trust that Anthony had in him paid big dividends for Trey and for the team. Grant looked back at that transition. "When I came in he was a guy who needed to mature and needed to grow up in some areas," he said. "We had some pretty open and honest conversations. We were able to connect, and our staff did a great job of connecting with him. So even when there were some bumps in the road, he was able to respect what we were asking of him." I look back on that fateful night in August when Trey was racing out the back door of Ned Pepper's with a crazed gunman pushing toward the front door.

Landers was the only Dayton native on the team, and he came to embody the Dayton Strong spirit that became a rallying cry for the Flyers and the community. Nancy Wilson from K99.1 FM hosts the pre-game show before home games. Included are interviews with the players, not so much about stats and facts, but their background and lives off the court. Trey told the story of how he and his brother Robert, who was a standout defensive tackle at Ohio State, told their mother they planned to be famous athletes. She had them practice doing interviews into a wooden spoon so they wouldn't sound stupid when that day came. Not only did Trey Landers have the loudest voice on the Flyers, but it was well-spoken. He delighted fans and media with his candor and passion. Brooks Hall shared the pride I felt in Trey's path to success. "Trey is probably the one player I have come closest to in terms of relationships in my life after playing at Dayton," he told me. "To watch his growth from his freshman year when he would open up to me about his struggles and his playing time—those kinds of things—and then to see how mature he was the last couple of years. He was the absolute leader on this team. He was the alpha, no question about it. I couldn't be prouder of him."

The Flyers had a few days to rest their legs. As regular-season champs, Dayton and the second-, third-, and fourth-place finishers drew first-round byes. The team flew to Brooklyn on Wednesday, March 11, and would play until Friday, March 13, at noon, against the winner of the Thursday noon game between VCU and UMass. The flight to New York was reminiscent of the trip to Maui. The coaches and staff had their wives and children with them. I sat with Security Man Michael Galbraith across from Darren Hertz and his family, and I talked to his son and daughter about how their basketball season had turned out. However, the trip already was lacking some of the festive feel of the previous days. That afternoon the A-10 announced that the tournament would be held without spectators. The rising global pandemic of the coronavirus that was now beginning to impact the United States was causing a growing apprehension not only in the sports world, but throughout the country. Out of caution, only a select few family members and friends would be allowed to attend the games. Some of the people from the UD Development Office who were there to coordinate pep rallies and other events involving boosters and alums grabbed commercial flights to head back to Dayton almost immediately upon landing.

That night we had what has become an annual gathering of sports information directors and radio broadcasters in the A-10. Kale Beers, who wears many hats at La Salle, including radio play-by-play, organized the get-together at a Mexican restaurant not far from where the Flyers were staying. Josh Postorino had flown from Phoenix, having planned on seeing some donors while in New York City and also working alongside me for our broadcasts. In addition to La Salle, Ray Goss and Jarrett Durham from Duquesne were there. "I feel so bad for you guys," Ray said. "Your fans always travel so well and for them not to be able to go to the games, and especially the kind of year you are having, that's just tragic." "Our guys are used to not playing in front of fans," piped in a member of the La Salle group. We continued chatting about our respective teams, the tournament, and if this whole "coronavirus thing" was going to get serious. As we were doing so, an NBA game between the Dallas Mavericks and Denver Nuggets was on in the background. Play stopped and there was a discussion involving both coaches at the scorer's table, and then the game continued. We could read on the crawl that Rudy Gobert and Donavan Mitchell, members of the Utah Jazz, had tested positive for the coronavirus, and the game between the Jazz and Oklahoma Thunder was suspended. By the time Josh and I walked back to the hotel, NBA Commissioner Adam Silver had suspended play effective at the end of the night's games.

The A-10 tournament has brought with it a variety of emotions for the Dayton Flyers and their fans through the years. Desperation—knowing that a tourney championship was the only path to the NCAA tournament. Anticipation—using a few tournament wins to complete a résumé worthy of an at-large bid. Even though Dayton went to Pittsburgh as outright champs in 2017, the A-10 tourney was almost an afterthought. This year it felt different. The Flyers and their fans were eagerly awaiting the chance to add another piece of hardware to the trophy case. The limitation of fans dampened enthusiasm, but not the team's resolve.

With most A-10 Championship memories involving disappointment on the court, Josh Postorino and I visited a familiar location for breakfast on the morning of March 12, where we had fond memories of good meals and a unique Brooklyn vibe. Junior's Restaurant and Bakery on Flatbush Avenue was founded in 1950. While known for their cheesecake, they also serve a great breakfast, lunch, and dinner. Josh and I did not need to decide to have breakfast there, but just what time, before we headed to the Barclays Center. It had been our experience in the previous years that Junior's on game day looked like a collage of fans wearing the gear of their favorite A-10 team. That day, it was nearly empty. No fans to be seen, since none were allowed at the tournament, and our fellow diners consisted of a few scattered tables of locals.

After breakfast we walked to the Barclays Center where the eerie post-apocalyptic feel continued. Normally the plaza outside would be packed with fans milling about, but again it was empty. We went inside, got our credentials, and arrived courtside within a few minutes of tip-off between UMass and VCU. Dayton would play the winner the next day at noon. Typically for the weekday afternoon games, the stands are packed with local elementary school kids who get out of class, are encouraged to make noise, and help create an atmosphere for the event. No kids. No noise. The only sounds were coming from the UMass and

VCU pep bands. Behind each bench was a smattering of fans and families of players and coaches. The teams finished warming up and the horn sounded to send them to their respective benches. The PA announcer greeted the "crowd" and was about to introduce the starting lineups, when he stopped. League officials were talking to him, and soon the two head coaches, Matt McCall of UMass and Mike Rhodes of VCU, were called over. As he left that meeting, Rhodes turned to the group of fans behind the VCU and acknowledged them, clapping his hands. It was then the PA announcer said:

> Ladies and Gentlemen, the 2020 Atlantic Ten Championship has been canceled. Please drive safely.

Josh looked back on that moment. "It still doesn't seem real to me. I went to Brooklyn a little worried about COVID-19 but not really about canceling games," he recalled. "When they canceled fans, I was disappointed but sure that the tourney would still happen. Then it just snowballed and went from 0 to 100 really quick. I will never forget us watching the warmups at the Barclays and them canceling the tournament right before our eyes. The teams didn't know what to do, they just kind of hung out. Actually a few of the seniors from UMass and VCU went and tried to make their last basket as college basketball players. We sat there in amazement and dazed at what just happened. 'Shocked' is an understatement. Brooklyn would become the epicenter for the pandemic in the world, and we were there in the thick of it at the very beginning."

Even though word came out earlier in the week that fans would not attend the tournament, Jeff Gonya told me his wife Leslie's travel group was still there in New York. "We had 61 people booked and 52 ended up going. Most of the people then just wanted to go home, but 11 flew back with us on Sunday."

As much as Josh and I were stunned by the announcement, we saw it coming. Other conferences had canceled their tournaments, and there was already talk that the NCAA would be played without fans, including the First Four in Dayton. We crossed the street to an Irish bar that had been scheduled to be the pregame and post-game gathering spot for Dayton fans. Those events had been canceled, and now the games as well. We had a sandwich and a few beers while watching the Big East tournament on TV above the bar. It was being played across the river at Madison Square Garden. At halftime of the game between Creighton and Saint John's, the Big East canceled its championship. Josh and I got word then from UD Director of Basketball Operations James Haring that we needed to get back to the hotel for a 5:00 departure for the airport. "It was tough for everybody," James recalled. "Over the course of four or five weeks leading up to the tournament in Brooklyn I had been planning for 1) being in New York, and 2) the contingencies of where we might be sent in the NCAA Tournament."

In looking back at memories of A-10 tournaments, one of the worst feelings is checking out of the hotel after being eliminated. I thought there was no worse feeling than packing a suitcase and taking a quiet ride to the airport, for an equally quiet ride on the plane, to be followed by more somber feelings en route back to campus. Fortunately, in recent years, A-10 disappointment has been assuaged by the promise of more games to come. However, the feeling of dread, and really just the lack of hope, that I felt as I gathered up my suitcase and radio gear is unsurpassed by anything I have felt in thirty-nine seasons of Flyer basketball.

Like any trip, you want to snap your fingers and be home, but the bus ride through New York traffic to the Teterboro Airport in New Jersey seemed like an eternity. Once we finally got on board the charter plane, everyone got on their phones and soon we all learned the inevitable, horrible news. Ryan Mikesell got word from his parents, who had been driving to New York. Rodney Chatman received a similar message. "My dad, mom, and little brother were on the way to Brooklyn when we all got the news," he recalled.

By the time the wheels were up on the plane, everyone knew. There would be no NCAA Tournament. No postponement. No games without fans. No revisiting the issue in a month. It was over. The Dayton Flyers season was done.

After returning to campus, Coach Grant addressed the team. "It was tough," he reflected. "We were dealing with a lot of emotion, raw emotion after something that transpired in six hours. Know that the group wasn't able to finish what it was committed to. We were laser-focused on winning an A-10 Championship plus knowing we had something bigger to play for after that. To have it taken away in a matter of hours was devastating."

Soon, thereafter though, Coach Grant addressed the Flyer Faithful via social media:

> Certainly we sit here disappointed that the season has ended in such an abrupt fashion, but without doubt the best thing for the safety and well-being of our players, our staff, all of our supporters and families, we feel

like the right decision was made. We thank you guys for all you did. For the environment you created at the UD Arena this year. All the support you showed us, whether we were at home or on the road. You made this place what we have always known, one of the best environments in college basketball.

In the next few days there was speculation that the NCAA Tournament committee would release a bracket, even though there would be no games played. For the Dayton Flyers it could have been validation that they had achieved a No. 1 seed. Many coaches, both head coaches and assistants, could qualify for bonuses if their teams had "made" the NCAA Tournament. But on the other hand, some hot seats could have warmed more for coaches whose schools were not on that final list of 68. Wisely, there was no bracket released and everyone was left to wonder, "what if."

Just a few days before the announcement in Brooklyn, on March 7, 2020, the Dayton Flyers cut down the nets at the UD Arena following a 76–51 win over George Washington. The outright Atlantic 10 Champions had a perfect 18–0 league mark, an overall record of 29–2, and had won 20 games in a row. And then it was over.

**Ryan Mikesell cuts down the nets
following win over George Washington**

19

THE GREATEST SEASON

FRIDAY, MARCH 13, 2020, THE DAYTON Flyers were back on campus feeling empty inside, as did anyone who was associated with the team, and certainly the Flyer Faithful across the nation. What would have been a Selection Sunday Show on WHIO Radio, was instead a post-mortem on the season. Keith Waleskowski joined me in studio for the two-hour show. Before that, I stopped at Milano's on Brown Street to get some pizzas to take in for Keith, me, and the producers working that night. A few somber Flyer fans that I knew were at the bar, with their grieving over the abrupt end of the season exacerbated by the fact that starting in a few hours, restaurants and bars would be closed for indoor dining, as a stay-at-home quarantine went into effect. The coronavirus pandemic which caused the sports world to come to a screeching halt was now isolating people from each other, left alone with their thoughts and in some cases little human contact to provide solace and comfort.

Almost immediately, Coach Grant stepped in and recorded a PSA, along with his wife, Chris, that was shown throughout Ohio, urging people to stay at home and be safe. I ran into Grad Assistant Khyle Marshall at the grocery store on Monday, March 16. He and I both felt an empty feeling. A trip to the grocery store was the only item on our to-do list on a day in which he would have been breaking down video on an opponent in the NCAA Tournament and I would have been securing credentials and getting rights fee checks cut and sent overnight. Coach Grant had told Khyle and the rest of the staff to just go home. A team that had accomplished incredible things on the court, due largely to their togetherness, were now separated, with communication limited to Zoom meetings, Face-Time, texts, and phone calls.

In the weeks that followed in which games would have been played, college basketball began handing out its post-season honors. On March 11, the day the Flyers left for New York, Obi Toppin was named a First Team *Sporting News* All-American. The following Monday he was named CBSSports.com National Player of the Year and the same organization named Anthony Grant National Coach of the Year. On March 20, Obi was named a First Team AP All-American and was the only unanimous selection. The US Basketball Writers (of which I am a member) also made Toppin a First Team All-American. That same day the AP made Toppin and Grant the National Player and Coach of the Year. The US Basketball Writers then gave out the Oscar Robertson Award for Player of the Year and the Henry Iba Award for Coach of the Year.

Bucky Bockhorn, who had been a teammate of Oscar in the NBA, was asked to call Obi and give him the news. "I told him, 'Obi, you are in high cotton,'" said Bucky. "'You are being compared to Oscar Robertson, who in my day was our Michael Jordan!'"

Don Donoher, who knew Henry Iba from his early coaching career, gave the word to Grant. "He was typical Anthony," Donoher told me. "He wasn't overly excited."

The National Association of Basketball Coaches then gave Toppin and Grant their top awards. Then the big ones came out. Obi was named to the Wooden All-American team, and then he and Grant were Naismith National Player and Coach of the Year. Obi Toppin and Anthony Grant had swept the major national awards.

While national acclaim is important, perhaps what really matters are the thoughts of those closest to the program. "Obi did something amazing every day at practice. It was never a dull day," said Rodney Chatman. "Sometimes I would throw it too high, because I assumed he would be able to go get it."

Obi had a presence on the University of Dayton campus as well as the UD Arena. "He was the same person on and off the court," said manager Henry Stark. "I would be walking across campus with some friends and we would see Obi and they would say, ask him if we can get a picture with him. I told them, ask him yourself, he's just a good guy. He'll do it."

Assistant Coach Ricardo Greer had "discovered" Obi and recruited him to Dayton. He said his breakout National Player of the Year season began as a redshirt his freshman year. "He was phenomenal. He understood that what it was going to take. He wanted to win games. He sat through a 14–17 season. I'm so proud of his effort. He always wanted to learn, to get better. He was always asking questions. He wants to please. That's why he looks over at Coach Grant when he makes a mistake."

For his part, Coach Grant was pleased. "A young man that wanted desperately the chance to continue the game that he loved. His appreciation and his gratitude for having an opportunity to be at Dayton. Just who he is, his character, his work ethic, his willingness to buy in to what our staff was asking him to do, the type of teammate his is, I think it's all a part of who he is," Grant told me. "The work that he put in that redshirt year, on the court, in the weight room, in the classroom and in the film room really helped him to be prepared. Throughout that process to see him remain true to be a humble, hard-working coachable young man and to see what he has become is probably what I appreciate the most."

And the coach who spent a time-out quietly teaching his star player about the importance of time, score, and motivating an opponent after Obi's between-the-legs-windmill dunk vs. Georgia Southern could still appreciate his incredible skill and athleticism. "There were several plays you go back and look at film and you laugh and say that was pretty special, some of the things he did." However, Grant said there were big-picture things that set Obi apart. "Not only a good teammate but the way he reacted with kids, adults and fans," he said. "And even fans on the road who would try to give him the business during the game, and then afterwards ask him for an autograph."

I remember, in particular, the Richmond baseball team, taunting him throughout warm-ups and during the game, only to congratulate him after the Flyer victory. I have seen lots of players either have "rabbit ears" and respond poorly to things they hear from the seats and trash-talking opponents. I have also seen great players succeed because they played with tunnel vision, shutting out the noise. Obi fed off the crowd, both good and bad, and was able to multi-task his focus.

Grant saw a similar ability in one of the players he coached with the NBA's Oklahoma City Thunder. "Russell Westbrook is the same way," Grant said. "There's a gym with 15 people and he'll say, 'hey, those are the same shoes you had on yesterday,' and to another guy, 'you cut your hair,' and to someone else, 'I heard what you said over there.'"

For some of the Flyer Faithful reading this, prepare for what you might think is blasphemy. I believe Obi Toppin is the most popular player in Dayton basketball history. Yes, even more popular than the charismatic Roosevelt Chapman. Who knows, perhaps if he had played for four years, Obi could have eclipsed Velvet as the Flyers all-time leading scorer. I ran that by Coach Grant, who shook his head and gave me an eye roll, maybe because Roosevelt was his teammate. Maybe because Chap scored 51 against Grant in Anthony's first scrimmage as a freshman. While Grant may not think his player has outshone his former teammate, Grant's former coach might.

I asked Don Donoher if he thought Obi was more popular with the fans than Roosevelt. "He's earned it," Donoher told me. "He has played at such a high level and he's a great teammate and a leader."

Roni Toppin told me she felt that the love the Flyer Faithful had for her son culminated in the season-finale vs. George Washington. "Throughout the game fans were coming up to me and thanking me for sharing my son, and would talk about how Obi and his teammates had helped them get through some tough times," she recalled. "They made me feel like a superstar."

As accolades rolled in from his peers and pundits, praise for Coach Grant also came from within. Anthony Solomon is the Associate Head Coach. "I was impressed with Coach Grant," he said. "We didn't compromise our principles that first year. He stayed with his vision for what the program was to be all about." Solomon also had the unenviable task of trying to restrain his muscular head coach during the heat of battle to prevent Grant from getting a technical. "There's an art to that," he said. "I have to show a certain level of calmness. If I am wrestling too hard with him, it looks like we are out of control."

To his star player, Grant was more than a coach. "He was like another father," Obi Toppin told me. "He put in the effort to make sure that I was good. He wanted everyone to succeed. He was pushing me every day when I sat out."

Grant impacted more than the elite players on his roster. Camron Greer made the team as a walk-on in AG's first year at Dayton. "Resiliency, leadership, consistency, and patience are what I learned most from Coach Grant and his staff," Greer told me. "I mean, think about it: here comes a coach that returns to coach for his alma mater after recently being fired. Having a losing record your first year is not easy to come back from. Despite that and the backlash as a result, the coaching staff coached with the same style and by the same principles no matter what. It definitely didn't get better overnight. Yet when everyone bought into the system that Coach Grant insisted and demanded for the program, success was bound to reveal itself eventually."

Fellow walk-on Christian Wilson echoed those sentiments. "From Coach Grant, personally, I have learned how to be successful in life in general," Wilson said. "You have to 'be about what we say we are about,' and this applies in all aspects of life. If you want to win a championship you must do all the little things all the time. He also taught how important it is to get along with your teammates to be successful. You should want to see your brothers shine which builds good chemistry."

That chemistry resulted in one of the elite offenses in the country in 2019–2020. While going 29–2, the Flyers led the nation in field goal percentage at 52.5% and were third in the nation in assists per game at 17.6, trailing Michigan State with 17.7 and Belmont with 18.3. The unselfishness and ball movement were a thing of beauty. "They had really smart seniors, and Jalen was so good at understanding how to score and when to pass," observed Josh Postorino. "They evolved with their basketball IQ when teams tried to keep Obi from beating them. Rodney got a little hard-headed at times, but those other guys understood the game. Obi impressed me with how he continued to understand how to play. They focused on scouting reports and keys to winning like it was a senior roster."

Ryan Mikesell says the style of play suited who they were. He remarked,

> I give the coaching staff credit for their ability to simplify it and allow us to focus on just a few things. We had a really good basketball IQ. Plus, they constantly asked us for our advice and opinion on how to approach certain situations. We all just clicked. No one was about themselves. This group shared a common goal. We enjoyed success together, so everyone as an individual had success. It was a read-and-react offense. Just because you have a good shot doesn't mean someone else doesn't have a great shot.

Brooks Hall saw a variety of assets come together to form a strong union. "The veteran leadership combined with a once-in-a-lifetime talent," he opined. "Dayton may never see an Obi Toppin again. When you have leadership with Trey Landers and Ryan Mikesell and of course Jalen Crutcher, combined with the skill set of Obi, you're going to have a poised ballclub that will figure out ways to win big games."

The overriding principle that guided everything the Flyers did was the culture of the program. Coach Grant's mantra is: "You don't get the culture you talk about. You get the culture you tolerate." Don Donoher was not surprised to see Anthony draw a figurative line in the sand upon arriving at UD. "Anthony is strong with his convictions," the Hall of Fame Coach told me. "I knew from day one there was soundness to his game plan for the program. That's the way he has always been." It was a culture in which players were valued as people first. Ibi Watson noticed the difference upon transferring from Michigan. "It was something not seen across the country," he told me. "They wanted us to be better players, better men, better people." Graduate Assistant Sean Damaska experienced something similar: "This was an exceptional group with a combination of senior leadership, veteran guys, and just guys who genuinely love each other and are glad to be around each other," he said. "I could see the seeds of success when I first got here. It was just a matter of getting everyone to buy in and to install trust in the process."

The Flyers made a powerful impression on the college basketball world and were a source of pride for Atlantic 10 Commissioner Bernadette McGlade. "Dayton's men's basketball teams' ascent to a No. 3 national ranking culminating with an undefeated conference regular season championship at 18–0 was historic," she said. "The university, Atlantic 10 Conference and Flyer Nation were energized, focused, and optimistic that the road to the Final Four would be a fun ride! The 2019–20 UD season will have historical significance for the A-10 and Dayton because of the teams' impressive record of success and the heartbreak of the COVID-19 pandemic that forced a screeching halt to competing for an A-10 Championship followed by a run to the national championship."

Ohio Governor Mike DeWine, whose father "took me to games in the old field house and I still have some old Flyer posters with pictures of Arlen Bockhorn and teammates that say: 'hear all the games on WHIO radio'" had a chance to come to the Arena for a few games. "It was a magical season that ended much too soon," he said. "We will never know for sure how far they would have gone, but we do know how very good they were. I have been a Flyer fan since the [Coach] Tom Blackburn era, have seen some great teams and players, but this Flyer team was as fun to watch as any I can remember."

The culture that directly led to so much success on the basketball court is helping the Flyers cope with having their post-season dreams shattered by the coronavirus pandemic. "When I heard that the NBA was canceled, I was hoping we could squeeze out a few more games," remembered Ibi Watson. "It was very emotional when Coach Grant told us, but I am grateful for what we were able to do. I was grateful that we were able to expand our relationships and put on a show for the whole country."

It was an especially painful ending for the collegiate career of Ryan Mikesell. "As time goes by, I have a better perspective about the importance of what we sacrifice for the greater good," Ryan explained to me. "There's a reason behind everything to happens, so you just control what you can. There is an emptiness, wanting to know "what if." I'm grateful for the time we had and I'm glad we were able to give the community something."

For Obi Toppin, who declared for the NBA draft and will be a no-doubt first-round pick, it marked an end to his days in a Flyer uniform. "I'm grateful for what we have accomplished. I think about 'what if' every day. We put our names on the map. Jalen was with me in Brooklyn for a few days and when we go out, people would say—'those are the two guys from Dayton.'"

Members of the staff felt themselves trying to cope with something that no game plan or scouting report could overcome. "Initially it was very challenging, and I will be wondering thirty years from now, how deep we could have gone in the tournament, if we could have won it all," Assistant Coach Darren Hertz told me during quarantine. "I felt so bad for our guys. To make a run in the NCAA Tournament is something special to be a part of. AG helped me get through it. Let us be grateful."

Grant was the leader in the aftermath, just as he had been during the record-setting season. "We created a lot of great memories over the year that won't be forgotten," he said. "We needed to be grateful for what we accomplished and the experience. Dayton basketball is bigger than any one season or any individual."

Grateful. How many times did that word come up when I asked members of the program about how they were dealing with the loss of a postseason, the loss of perhaps a national championship? It is no coincidence that word is used and how it has become a word of healing for the Flyers. At the end of every practice the team gathers on the court, holding hands in a circle. If I am there, I am asked to join. If former Flyers are there visiting, they are asked to join. If the team is on the road and a CBS or ESPN broadcast crew is there watching practice, they are asked to join. And someone begins, sharing with the group what they are grateful for. Rarely is basketball addressed, other than to show gratitude to be together as teammates or being played in a wonderful place like Maui. After a few people speak, practice ends. A small thing, perhaps, done daily gave the Dayton Flyers a foundation to deal with adversity—and instead of a lifetime of regret, they are sharing a lifetime of gratitude.

This Dayton Flyers team will be remembered for many things. Keith Waleskowski was alongside me for many of the radio broadcasts. "I will personally remember not necessarily what this team did, but how they did it," he shared with me. "The personality, character, and work ethic of the individuals on this team might never be matched. Yes, they were extremely fun to watch, but to know that on top of that, behind the scenes they were even better people makes me proud to be a Dayton Flyer!"

Another proud Dayton Flyer was Don Donoher. "I was impressed with their camaraderie," he told me. "It started with Obi. Having the main guy buy into the team concept was key. It's hard to get some of those personalities all pulling in the same direction, but Anthony got them to buy in. Night after night they would rise to the occasion when they had to execute. They had those spurts, where they would string together offensive possessions at important times with a rash of field goals. They believed in each other."

Bucky Bockhorn did not work any games with me during the season, but followed the team closely. "I will remember how unselfish they were," he said. "It was remarkable the way they would make the extra pass, and of course, they had a helluva coach!'"

Mike Galbraith had a unique perspective after traveling with the team to provide security on the road. "What an amazing run for me. Undefeated in all of those games, and no incidents," he recalled. "It was difficult not to cheer on the bench. Sometimes difficult to contain myself when I would see some of the plays these guys made. None of us working security had seen something so wonderful as this team. I was as proud as they were of this season."

Obi Toppin's mother, Roni, says one word can describe the 2019–2020 Dayton Flyers: *love*. "The bond they had was incredible," she told me after the season. "They loved to play the game and they were playing for him [Coach Grant)] for their teammates, for the fans. They wanted things to be as good for everyone else as it was for them."

Dayton Flyer basketball teams through the years have been judged largely by post-season success. Granted, it takes a successful regular season to even get to post-season play. However, if you are a die-hard Flyer Fan, as you are reading this and you recall great Flyer teams, the 1967 team that lost to UCLA in the NCAA Championship game will come to mind, as will the Elite Eight Teams of 1984 and 2014. Some of you will think back to NIT titles in 1962, 1968, and 2010. Many fans can remember beating West Virginia in 2009 to end a drought of NCAA tourney losses, but few can recall details of the season that got them there. The Flyers 2000 NCAA victory over Illinois in the NCAA tourney in Austin came after a ten-game winning streak. Some great regular seasons have been overshadowed by early post-season exits. The 1955–56 Flyers were ranked third in the nation after beating the host Wildcats in the University of Kentucky Invitational, ended the season 25–3, and then lost in the first round of the NIT to the hated Xavier Muske-teers. Oliver Purnell's final year saw Dayton enter the NCAA Tournament as a four seed, only to be upset by 13th seed Tulsa in Spokane. The Flyers won back-to-back A-10 regular season championships in 2016 and 2017. However, they were one-and-done in the NCAA, losing to Syracuse and then Wichita State.

The 2019–2020 Dayton Flyers did not have a postseason to either bolster their legacy or tarnish it. So how will this edition of Dayton basketball be not just remembered, but judged? I maintain it was the greatest season in Dayton basketball history, and I will not qualify my opinion by saying "regular season." The numbers speak for themselves. Twenty-nine wins is a school record. An 18–0 mark had not been ac-complished since the A-10 went back to an 18-game league schedule. The 20-game winning streak was the longest in a single season in school history. The Flyers were undefeated on the road for the first time since 1954–55. And an unofficial record of sorts—with their only losses coming in overtime to Kansas and Colorado—Dayton was the first NCAA Division I basketball team to go undefeated in regulation since the 1975–76 National Champion Indiana Hoosiers. For the first time in school history, Dayton boasted the consensus National Player and Coach of the Year.

The numbers tell only part of the story. The 2019–2020 Dayton Flyers racked up those wins with class, character, and camaraderie. They stood as a beacon of coming together and sacrificing for the greater good, at a time when the Dayton community was reeling from the devastating Memorial Day tornadoes and the horrific Oregon District Shootings. There is no doubt in my mind that on winter evenings, wheth-er getting LOWD in the UD Arena, listening to the radio, or gathered around a TV, people felt better about themselves and their lives by watching young men who truly cared about each other and played with a palpable joy and love for the game.

The coronavirus pandemic did not allow the Dayton Flyers to write the final chapter of their story. Sitting here, seeking to put the right words to paper, I cannot write that final chapter either. It will be written over time by the people who remember this season, not the what-ifs, but what was. The final chapter will be a feeling of gratitude for who they are, what they did, and the men who guided them.

Let us be grateful for the greatest season. The Dayton Flyers . . . bigger than basketball.

.